TIME-LIFE BOOKS

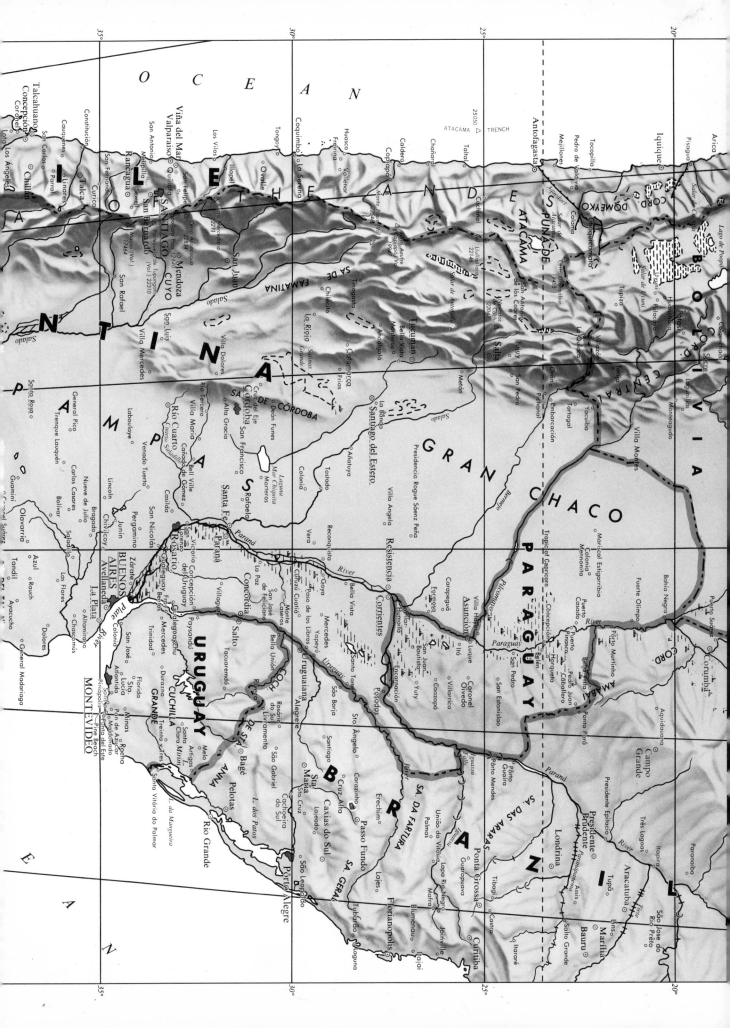

LIFE WORLD LIBRARY

THE RIVER PLATE REPUBLICS

ARGENTINA, PARAGUAY, URUGUAY

by J. Halcro Ferguson

and The Editors of LIFE

A STONEHENGE BOOK

TIME INCORPORATED   NEW YORK

COVER: An Argentine couple, wearing
the traditional loose scarves
of the Gauchos, ride with their dog
to market in the hilly Bariloche
region of western Patagonia.

ABOUT THE WRITER

J. Halcro Ferguson, author of the interpretive text for this volume of the LIFE
World Library, has been Latin American correspondent for the London weekly
newspaper *The Observer* since 1948. In that capacity Mr. Ferguson has visit-
ed, and written about, virtually every country in Latin America. Before joining
The Observer he served in the British Foreign Office for a number of years, being
attached to the British embassy in Buenos Aires from 1941 to 1946, and then to the
embassy in Bogotá, Colombia. In addition to his articles for *The Observer*, Mr.
Ferguson has written on Latin American subjects for *The New Statesman* and *The
Spectator* and a number of other British publications as well as for Argentine,
Mexican and Chilean journals. He has also broadcast on the BBC and on several
Latin American stations. Mr. Ferguson has written two books on Latin American
subjects: *Latin America: The Balance of Race Redressed* and *The Revolutions of
Latin America*. Born of Scottish parents in 1920, and a graduate of Cambridge
University, Mr. Ferguson lives with his wife in a village in Surrey, England.

Contents

TIME-LIFE BOOKS

EDITOR
Norman P. Ross
TEXT DIRECTOR   ART DIRECTOR
William Jay Gold   Edward A. Hamilton
CHIEF OF RESEARCH
Beatrice T. Dobie
Assistant Text Director: Jerry Korn
Assistant Chief of Research: Monica O. Horne
•

PUBLISHER
Rhett Austell
General Manager: Joseph C. Hazen Jr.
Business Manager: John D. McSweeney
Circulation Manager: Joan D. Manley

LIFE MAGAZINE

EDITOR: Edward K. Thompson
MANAGING EDITOR: George P. Hunt
PUBLISHER: Jerome S. Hardy

LIFE WORLD LIBRARY
SERIES EDITOR: Oliver E. Allen
Editorial Staff for *The River Plate Republics:*
Assistant Editor: David S. Thomson
Designer: Ben Schultz
Chief Researcher: Grace Brynolson
Researchers: Sondra Albert, Rebecca Chaitin, Evelyn Hauptman,
Donald Newton, Louise Samuels, Ruth Silva,
Rosemarie Tauris Zadikov, Edward Brash

EDITORIAL PRODUCTION
Art Associate: Robert L. Young
Art Assistants: James D. Smith, John M. Woods
Picture Researchers: Margaret K. Goldsmith, Barbara Sullivan
Copy Staff: Marian Gordon Goldman, Patricia Miller,
Dolores A. Littles

The interpretive text for this book was written by J. Halcro Ferguson
and the picture essays were written by George Constable. Many of the
photographs were taken by Leonard McCombe, LIFE staff photogra-
pher. Valuable help was provided by the following individuals and departments of Time Incorporated: Doris O'Neil, Chief, LIFE Picture
Library; Content Peckham, Chief, Bureau of Editorial Reference;
Richard M. Clurman, Chief, TIME-LIFE News Service; Gavin Scott of
the Buenos Aires Bureau; Alberto R. Cellario, Associate Editor of LIFE
EN ESPAÑOL; Eva Candia and Carlos J. Vega of LIFE EN ESPAÑOL.

Introduction

In the year 1945 a high official of the Export-Import Bank of Washington visited Asunción for the first time. After walking around Paraguay's pocket-sized capital and looking into the eyes of Paraguayans, he said to a companion, "I hope nothing we may do will change these people."

Geography has seen to it that Paraguayans have changed little. Tucked away in South America's heartland, far from centers of population of other countries, politically volatile Paraguay has probably changed more slowly than any other South American country. And yet it is moving ahead. On the other hand, Uruguay and Argentina, its two neighbors in the River Plate area, while they have far outdistanced Paraguay in political and material progress, today are advancing only slowly, if at all.

Uruguay has had outstanding success among Latin American countries in developing and preserving democratic institutions; indeed, it created a "welfare state" in which its citizens take a considerable measure of pride. But it has had less success in meeting contemporary economic problems.

Argentina, a country of vast distances and vast resources, containing one of the richest agricultural areas of the world, needs only stable politics and rational economic policies to move rapidly toward world-power status. But it has had little of either in recent years. The coup d'état has become a favorite device for changing governments, and governmental economic decisions too often have been based on ideological rather than economic considerations.

The Perón Government spent over half a billion dollars of much-needed foreign exchange in purchasing the country's railroads from their British owners. These railroads have been featherbedded to an outrageous degree, and their operating losses are responsible for a very large part of Argentina's massive and chronic budgetary deficit, with its melancholy sequel of inflation, reduced confidence on the part of the economic community, and political and social strife.

The Frondizi Government rescued Argentina from imminent economic disaster but was overturned by force in 1962, and the Illia regime arbitrarily canceled the Frondizi Government's contracts with foreign oil companies—although the companies had contributed to making Argentina substantially self-sufficient in petroleum.

Perhaps troubles such as these will be vanquished in the near future. Certainly the River Plate countries will grow in population and in prosperity with the years. They have the material resources and, even more importantly, the human resources required for growth. Paraguay will find itself hoping to become a little more acquainted with the outside world, and the world with Paraguay. And of course Paraguayans will have to learn to get along better with each other. Uruguay and Argentina will move ahead rapidly when they face more candidly the problems that plague them in today's complex and interdependent world.

The people of Paraguay, Uruguay and Argentina have many qualities in common with North Americans, and what happens in those countries will have great importance for the United States. What happens, in turn, will depend in great measure on the kind of cooperation the three countries achieve with the United States and with other countries with which they have political and economic ties. That cooperation will be fruitful to the degree that it is based on reciprocal knowledge and understanding. The Editors of LIFE and Mr. Ferguson have done us an important service in preparing this informative volume, which merits wide reading.

WILLARD L. BEAULAC
former U.S. Ambassador to Paraguay and to Argentina

Young mothers and children spend an afternoon in a Buenos Aires square shaded by the gnarled branches of an ombú tree, native to the

Argentine Pampa, and adorned with one of the city's many statues.

1

Three Nations Linked by Great Rivers

THE River Plate—which the Spanish-speaking people call the Río de la Plata—is one of the great waterways of the world, and like the Danube or the Mississippi, it has had a profound effect on the vast area that forms its basin. Yet, strictly speaking, it is not a river at all, but a wide estuary fed by the Uruguay and Paraná Rivers and their tributaries, and itself stretches only a little more than 150 miles between the confluence of its parent streams and the South Atlantic.

At first sight, as the visitor flies across it to come in to land at Ezeiza, Buenos Aires' international airport, the River Plate is curiously unimpressive, despite its width, at that point, of 20 miles. Slow and sluggish, it is not the color of silver, as its name implies, but a dark, muddy brown. The land on the northern, Uruguayan bank undulates so gently that its contours are barely perceptible from the air. From a height it looks like an improbably underpopulated part of the south of England—a tame and domesticated landscape. The land to the south, the Argentine Pampa, is as flat as the North American

GREAT RIVER SYSTEM of the Plate, second-largest of South America's inland waterway networks, connects the three countries of Argentina, Uruguay and Paraguay and creates one of South America's natural geographical divisions. The Pilcomayo River, which forms much of the Argentine-Paraguayan border, flows into the Paraguay. The Paraná River forms the eastern border of Paraguay, meets the Paraguay River and, paralleling the Uruguay River, flows southward into the River Plate. The wide Plate, although an estuary, has always been called a river—the Río de la Plata in Spanish—and since colonial times has given its name to the region covered in this volume. This river system remains the area's most vital commercial artery.

prairie. It is a checkerboard of vast, rectangular fields and pastures, the pattern varied only by the railroads and highways fanning out from Buenos Aires to the interior. To the disappointment of some romantic tourists, the vegetation is familiar—most of the trees, indeed, which march in straight lines to act as windbreaks and check soil erosion, belong to species imported from the Old World.

Approached from the sea, however, the wide estuary of the River Plate is a good deal more exciting. But the excitement, like that of the entrance to New York Harbor, is principally man-made. The only prominent natural feature is the Cerro, the conical hill that stands beside the Uruguayan capital, Montevideo, at the mouth of the Plate. Indeed, this modest hill gave the city its name: a Portuguese sailor is reputed to have called out on first sighting it, *"Monte vejo eu!"* (I see a mountain!), though even at the time the description must have seemed an exaggeration. Today the Cerro, topped by a lighthouse and symbolically guarded by ancient cannon,

is dwarfed by the buildings that now dominate the downtown section of Montevideo, which juts out in a narrow peninsula like a minor Manhattan, and by the great white blocks of luxury apartments and hotels that line the crowded, sandy beaches stretching away to the northeast.

Upstream 123 miles, off the port bow, Buenos Aires, Argentina's capital, first reveals itself as a dark smudge on the horizon even when the sky is unclouded blue—a graphic manifestation of the air pollution of a modern industrial city. Then gradually the tops of skyscrapers and the factory chimneys come into sight, and the ship enters port to dock within a few yards of the roaring traffic, dominated by huge trucks with trailers rumbling in from the pampas with produce for export.

Nearly 1,000 miles farther upstream, up the Paraná River and its main tributary, the Paraguay, past the great Argentine grain port of Rosario and past hundreds of small, riverside pueblos and the occasional large towns which line these rivers, lies Asunción, the sleepy, hot, humid, provincial-looking capital of Paraguay, the third of the River Plate republics.

These three countries, though united by their waterways, their history, their language, their religion and their culture, have nevertheless developed very separate identities.

Argentina is by far the largest of the three, with 1,072,000 square miles, stretching from the semitropics in the north to the Antarctic in the south, from the Cordillera (Backbone) of the Andes in the west to the South Atlantic in the east—an inverted triangle pointing to the South Pole. Paraguay—including the barely inhabited badlands of the Gran Chaco—boasts a mere 157,000 square miles. And temperate Uruguay, nestling at the southernmost end of huge Brazil, has only 72,000 square miles, not much larger than England and Wales. But the natural divisions within this huge region have little or no connection with present-day national frontiers.

THE largest of these natural divisions is the flat, fertile Pampa, a great plain stretching for hundreds of miles to the west and south of Buenos Aires. This area, entirely treeless—except for an occasional gigantic, treelike herb called the ombú—until the Spaniards brought European varieties with them, seems to the stranger almost frighteningly bare and monotonous. Even today, although the area is crisscrossed by highways and railroads and telegraph lines, dotted with towns and carved up into rectangular pastures, one can still gaze all around and see nothing between oneself and the horizon except perhaps a lonely line of thin wire fencing.

But to the Pampa-born the area is beautiful, and every Argentine, however city-bound, feels in himself an identification with this immensity. In his book *Historia de una Pasión Argentina*, the Argentine author Eduardo Mallea wrote: "This was the pampa, the far horizon, the prairie, the desert. . . . A few hundred meters away began the flat countryside under an unequalled sky. Human destinies disturbed no more, with their conversations and surprises, only the earth's dialogue with the clouds, the fate of the invisible wheat which grows from the fallen and reborn grain."

QUITE different, to the north, is the rolling countryside of the Argentine Province of Entre Ríos (so called because it lies between the Paraná and Uruguay Rivers) and the Oriental Republic of Uruguay (the country's official name, because it lies on the eastern, or "oriental," shore of the Uruguay River). Here the country is undulating and of more human dimensions; winding streams cross it, fringed by weeping willows. This was the region known to the Anglo-Argentine writer W. H. Hudson as "the purple land."

When Hudson wrote the book of that name in 1885, the region was as wild as the hard-riding, hard-drinking, proud and quarrelsome Gauchos who roamed it. Today it is tamed, crossed by macadam roads lined with poplars, traversed by sleek, long-distance buses, and dotted with small, neat houses and rolling ranches, or *estancias*—smaller and more intimate than those of the Pampa. It all bears some resemblance to parts of Normandy in France.

In the south of Uruguay, along the shores of the River Plate (here as wide as the English Channel, so that the Argentine shore is out of sight), the grasslands give way to sandy soil which nurtures woods of pine and eucalyptus running down to the long beaches, woods today honeycombed with discreetly hidden chalets owned by retired people and summer

vacationists. Here and there rise miniature mountains, like Pan de Azúcar (Sugar Loaf) behind the resort of Piriápolis, giving a welcome variety to the landscape. Everything here is on a small scale, accentuating the European atmosphere.

To the north of the purple land lies a lowland area covering part of Uruguay, the Argentine Provinces of Misiones and Corrientes, and the eastern part of Paraguay. Here one is almost in the tropics; though the winters (corresponding in time to the summers of the Northern Hemisphere) are comparatively mild, the summers are hot and humid. The temperate vegetation gives way to thick forest, the trees adorned and strangled with creepers; orchids grow here, and parrots and hummingbirds abound. Although in both the Paraguayan and the Argentine parts of this lowland region cattle are still reared, much of the area is given over to the cultivation of yerba, the plant that yields yerba maté, or Paraguayan tea, the traditional drink of all three River Plate countries.

Westward stretches the inhospitable Gran Chaco, part of it in northern Argentina, the other and major portion the scene of the bitter Paraguayan-Bolivian war of 1932 to 1935, to which Shakespeare's lines in *Hamlet* might well apply:

We go to gain a little patch of ground
That hath in it no profit but the name.
To pay five ducats, five, I would not farm it . . .

The difference is that the Chaco, far from being little, makes up about two thirds of present-day Paraguay. Lying to the west of the Paraguay River, the Chaco is a parched waste during the dry season, a swamp during the wet. While eastern Paraguay was described by early travelers as Arcadia, the Chaco has been likened to hell. A North American historian of the Chaco War, Captain David H. Zook Jr., has this to say of the area: "Westward to about 59° the region consists of extensive palm groves, high pastures, and small woods. Beyond there was not a town or place, however attractive the name, that was anything but a collection of mud huts. . . . [The Chaco proper] consists of arid desert, often clothed with thick scrub and brush. Here the juice of cacti replaces water, and blood-sucking insects swarm by the millions. When during the months of the southern summer the rains come to this land, the rough roads turn to quagmires; during the dry season the fine, powdery soil rises in great lingering clouds."

To the west and south of this inhospitable expanse lies the region of Argentina, stretching across several provinces, which is still sometimes known by its traditional name of Cuyo, centering on the wine-producing Province of Mendoza. The Cuyo affords a contrast to both the desert and jungle on the northeast and to the Pampa. Approaching by road or rail from Buenos Aires, one suddenly catches sight of the backdrop of the Andes, rearing against the horizon, appearing to grow higher and more menacing with every mile, bringing an abrupt stop to Argentina, like a natural Iron Curtain dividing the country from Chile on the other side.

Against this stern background lie the flowering foothill provinces, covered with purple vineyards and watered by wandering streams. This is the oldest settled part of the whole River Plate region, and with its tiled roofs and colonial churches it has an air of continuity and peace—though this, as with many peaceful-looking parts of Europe, is belied by its turbulent history.

TO the north of Mendoza lie the sugar-growing provinces; southward the Andes march down toward the Antarctic, and in the foothills are forests and inland lakes, making an Argentine Switzerland (as the travel brochures invariably point out). Between the mountains and the sea is an area long known as Patagonia, now divided into the Argentine Provinces of Neuquén, Río Negro, Chubut and Santa Cruz, and a national territory comprising half the island of Tierra del Fuego, the rest of which is owned by Chile. (The British-administered Falkland Islands and their dependent Antarctic Territory are also claimed by Argentina.)

Río Negro is a fruit-growing province, and Chubut is the center of the Argentine oil industry based on the wind-swept South Atlantic city of Comodoro Rivadavia. But, just as the Pampa's wealth comes from cattle and grain, that of Patagonia comes principally from sheep. Descendants of immigrants have made huge fortunes here, but they have done it the hard way, braving the rigors of snow-deep winters alternating with blazing, shadeless summers to establish and maintain their flocks.

At the foot of Argentina is Ushuaia, on the southern coast of Tierra del Fuego (which is divided from the mainland by the icy waters of the Strait of Magellan). Ushuaia claims the honor of being the southernmost town in the world. Until recently it was the site of a maximum-security prison; now it is only a naval base, and the most unpopular post in the Argentine armed forces.

SO far we have concerned ourselves almost exclusively with the River Plate countryside. But, except for Paraguay, today's Rioplatenses—people of the River Plate area—are overwhelmingly urban and suburban. Of Argentina's 22-odd million people, seven million—or about a third—live in Greater Buenos Aires alone. Of Uruguay's 2.6 million, about half live in Montevideo and its environs. What are these River Plate cities like?

By far the largest, of course, is Buenos Aires, whose full name proclaims it to be the city of Our Lady Holy Mary of the Fair Wind. This seductive label leads many people to believe that the city is an Argentine version of Rio de Janeiro, with golden beaches and palm trees and perhaps some mountains overlooking it. The reality is very different.

Apart from accessibility, the original settlement possessed no natural advantages when it was founded in 1536. Surrounded on three sides by the bare Pampa and on the fourth by the broad but muddy Río de la Plata (whose title, Silver River, referred not to its color, but to the merchandise that the conquistadors hoped to ship down it), Buenos Aires was, as will be seen later, the neglected Cinderella of the Spanish colonial empire. Only in the 18th and 19th Centuries, with the development of commerce, did the city begin to assume the size and importance it has today.

One result of this late development is that Buenos Aires is an almost entirely modern metropolis, with scarcely a vestige left of its colonial past. Unlike New York, it was built from the outset on a grid pattern, which the Spanish colonizers copied from the Romans, who had once colonized Spain, so that there are no crooked, curious downtown streets. The nearest approach to the pleasant disorder of

New York's Greenwich Village is the rather shabby district of La Boca, down by the old port, many of whose balconied houses are built unromantically of corrugated iron.

In the city's center, there are few buildings surviving from before the 19th Century. And even the most historic one of all, the Cabildo, or old Spanish town hall, where the first independent government of the area was established in 1810, has had both its ends lopped off to make way for a Parisian boulevard (the Avenida de Mayo) and one of the two diagonal avenues that have been cut through to facilitate the flow of traffic.

This is in its way symptomatic. The *porteños*, literally, "port dwellers," as the citizens of Buenos Aires are called, are an unsentimental people, and theirs is an unsentimental city. Although, as with the Avenida de Mayo, much of the 19th Century building was based on French models, Buenos Aires has none of the grace or relaxation of Paris. Past the somehow severe-looking sidewalk cafés the teeming pedestrians hurry with as much urgency as the cars and buses, and the streets run relentlessly block after block toward the Pampa, like visions of an inescapable eternity.

As befits such a city, five subway lines rumble beneath its surface, and there are six main railroad terminals, three of them next door to each other, all built by the British and looking like it. The few downtown open spaces are formal squares, with traffic passing on all sides of them, and in recent decades the sense of claustrophobia has been increased by the rising number of office buildings and apartment houses of 20 stories and more. Some 20 blocks inland from the port a wide avenue, the Nueve de Julio, the width of a city block, has been bulldozed through the city from north to south; it is impressive but cold, and some travelers say it reminds them of Moscow.

Not surprisingly, the majority of *porteños* live out of the city's center and commute to work. The city itself is separated from the Province of Buenos Aires by a semicircular motorway. Within the motorway are pleasantly Victorian, tree-lined areas; beyond the city limits the modern suburbs, largely English in style, with gardens and hedges and open

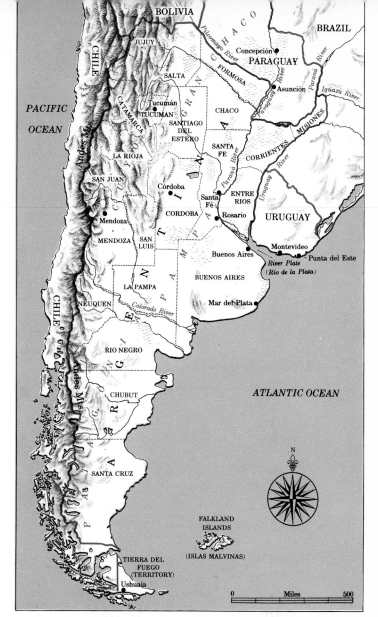

PRINCIPAL REGIONS of the River Plate area are shown above. Although Paraguay and Uruguay have administrative departments, these are not as significant as Argentina's provinces.

living-room fireplaces, stretch for 10 miles and more into the Pampa. In the south of the city are the crowded working-class *conventillos*, or tenements; and in recent years the influx of *campesinos*, or rural people, has led to the growth of shantytowns called *villas miseria* around the metropolitan periphery. *Porteños* love their city, and many immigrants, whether from the provinces or from Europe, grow to do so, but it is an acquired taste—though once acquired, not lost.

If Buenos Aires is the undisputed great metropolis of the River Plate region, Montevideo, the capital of Uruguay, the only city to approach it in size and elegance, is the region's little metropolis. And though it is separated from its sister city by only 40 minutes' flying time, and comings and goings are as constant as between New York and Philadelphia, the two cities are worlds apart in atmosphere. In some indefinable way, they even *smell* different, and anyone knocked out in Buenos Aires and taken to Montevideo would know immediately upon regaining consciousness that he was in Uruguay.

Compared with Buenos Aires, Montevideo is a peaceful place. Life proceeds more slowly, sounds are less strident, and the whole atmosphere is, in no offensive sense, a more provincial one. This is not to say that Montevideo is in any way old-fashioned. True, it lacks subways, but its municipal and its cooperatively owned buses provide a rather better service than the surface transport of Buenos Aires. Again, although the city is short on actual skyscrapers, apart from the beloved but hideous Palacio Salvo and the equally hideous Hotel Victoria Plaza, the modern apartment houses along the beaches of suburban Pocitos make a little Copacabana.

But in spite of these innovations, and bars describing themselves improbably as *whiskerías*, Montevideo has an air of solidity and even antiquity which Buenos Aires somehow lacks. The narrow streets of the downtown peninsula, which was the original center of the city, still have an Old World air. The cathedral still dominates the Plaza Matriz, as it did in the days before independence—and people still call the square Plaza Matriz, despite the fact that for more than a century the signs have read Plaza Constitución.

I F Montevideo is a small metropolis, Asunción, the capital of Paraguay, is little more than a large provincial capital. Civilian life is slower, simpler, more friendly and more leisured than almost anywhere else in the River Plate area, although Paraguay's old military tradition makes itself felt in a frequency of bugle calls and marching men. The suburbs of Asunción have a more relaxed look than those of either Buenos Aires or Montevideo, and the lawns have a more natural appearance, although they have no doubt been as assiduously mowed. Above all, there is less contrast in the size and opulence of dwellings. Virtually nobody in Asunción

is disproportionately rich. Even the Government Palace has been more than once mistaken for the Post Office. The erection of a modern hotel in the principal plaza has still failed—happily perhaps—to make Asunción look like a metropolis.

The three national capitals are far from being the only cities of consequence in the River Plate region. Several cities antedated them in importance and preserve an air of antiquity the capitals do not possess. In Uruguay, Maldonado, Treinta y Tres, Colonia and Paysandú—despite new building—are still dominated by the towers of churches; most of their houses are still of one tall story built around a patio; the plazas have still a colonial look; and markets continue to be more important than supermarkets.

I N Argentina the older cities—Córdoba, Tucumán, Santa Fe—are larger, busier and noisier than the old cities of Uruguay. Córdoba for one is now the center of the national automobile industry. But just as Oxford in England, although now an important automobile-manufacturing center, has managed to preserve its atmosphere of a cathedral and university city, so has Córdoba. Iconoclastic *porteños* have expressed the view that "all those dirty old buildings" should be pulled down. The *cordobeses* do not agree.

But during this century, the only old cities that have continued to prosper are those that, like Córdoba, have attracted industry to themselves or have benefited accidentally by a geographical position making them attractive to tourists. In the meantime, other municipalities, some with no claims to beauty or historical renown, have grown up by virtue of industry or because of political importance.

Statistically one of the largest cities in Argentina is Avellaneda, divided from Buenos Aires only by a murky strip of water called the Riachuelo. Large parts of it are reminiscent of the East End of London or the more unattractive parts of Jersey City, but the meat-packing plants and factories whose chimneys foul the air and whose waste products pollute the river provide work for thousands and are an essential part of the national economy. Ports like Rosario, though of much older foundation, also owe their pre-eminence to economic causes; while La Plata, capital of the Province of Buenos Aires (an hour south by train from the Federal Capital itself and founded only in 1882), is a city of civil servants.

To these comparatively new communities must be added those created in the late 19th Century and the 20th by increased wealth and leisure and by the international trend toward vacations by the sea or in the mountains. The first and still most famous of these resorts is Mar del Plata in Argentina, on the Atlantic coast 250 miles south of Buenos Aires, which attracts everyone from millionaires to garbage collectors. Its beach is as crowded as any from Coney Island to Cannes, and it is dominated by its huge casino. Some of the smarter boutiques in Buenos Aires move themselves bodily to Mar del Plata during the summer season, which gets under way just before Christmastime.

Rivaling Mar del Plata is the Uruguayan resort of Punta del Este. It is less urban than Mar del Plata, and nowadays more sophisticated and cosmopolitan, with a district whose streets are named after United States Presidents. Smaller resorts—Solís, Piriápolis, Atlántida—string along the shore between "Punta" and Montevideo, each with its own social cachet and clientele.

Finally, away from the sea and into the Andes, there is the luxurious resort of San Carlos de Bariloche in the southern Andes of Argentina, connected with the capital of Buenos Aires by frequent air flights and a railroad service. Beyond the purses of many Rioplatenses, Bariloche has become a center for international tourism.

BUT none of these places is typical. The average River Plate pueblo is a small town, situated on a main highway or railroad, marked out from afar by a silo or a white church tower. It is perhaps 5 blocks by 10 in size, but only a few of the streets are paved. There are neon signs along the *calle mayor,* or main street, and to the outsider the town is ugly and dull.

To the same outsider such towns all look exactly alike. But to their inhabitants each one is vastly different, and their own is certainly the best.

This parochial pride is paralleled by a similarly strong national feeling. Of all the Latin American countries, there are none more jealous of their separate sovereignty, more covetous of their traditions, more reverent to their national heroes (whatever these heroes' faults or inconsistencies) than are Argentina, Uruguay and Paraguay.

Yet a century and a half ago, when they were struggling for their independence from Spain, there seemed a good chance that the three of them would form one nation, continuing the association that they had under the Spanish Viceroyalty of the River Plate. Uruguay celebrates Argentina's national day (May 25) as well as its own (July 18). On both occasions the Argentine Ambassador has been known to share the balcony of Montevideo's old colonial town hall with the president of the Uruguayan Council of Government and the mayor of Montevideo.

APART from their historical affinities and the centripetal attraction of the city of Buenos Aires —which is the principal River Plate port—the three countries have been paradoxically united by their separation from everyone else. They are cut off by the Andes to the west, by the vast bulk of Portuguese-speaking Brazil to the north, and by the Atlantic Ocean and the Antarctic to the east and south.

Some of this sense of remoteness persists to this day. Rioplatenses, particularly Argentines, have a tendency to say "America" when they mean the River Plate area as a whole, to use "South America" for their immediate neighbors, and "Central America" (rather pejoratively) for anything between Peru and the United States border—while the U.S. itself is invariably *Norteamerica.*

But modern communications have done much to break down this regionalism. Perhaps even more important has been the influx of Old World immigrants who have poured into the River Plate countries since the middle of the last century, and who have modified the way of life in their new countries much more fundamentally than did their counterparts who went to the United States. Many immigrant groups arriving in the U.S. have tended to settle in particular communities—the Germans, for example, sticking to New York's Yorkville area, the Swiss to farms in Wisconsin. Immigrants to Argentina have on the whole been more widely dispersed and have intermarried more quickly. Thus their customs have rapidly spread through the whole community, giving the region a new and characteristic cosmopolitanism.

A Variegated Land That Dwarfs Its Conquerors

From the tropical forests of Paraguay to the bleak southern tip of Argentina, the River Plate countries embrace a striking diversity of climate and topography. As a result, the people have had to tame the land in many different ways. In the west, they have planted orchards and vineyards. In wind-swept Patagonia and on the Argentine Pampa, they have established cattle and sheep ranches. But the cities claim a high proportion of the people, and much of the land still has an empty, wild and untamable look.

A truckload of raw hides, one of Argentina's major exports, is readied for shipment from the port of Buenos Aires to Poland.

Workers harvest wine grapes in Mendoza Province, an agricultural area of western Argentina bordering on the Andes.

IMMENSE, ROLLING PLAIN stretches away beyond two Gauchos—the cowboys of the River Plate—who are herding sheep on a Uruguayan ranch. Most of Uruguay is covered by this grassy plain, and 80 per cent of the country's area is devoted to cattle and sheep grazing, while only 8 per cent is cultivated. There are some 21 million head of sheep in the country.

HUGE, SPRAWLING RANCH on the Argentine Pampa *(below)* is surveyed from a carriage by a landowner and his friends. The Pampa, Argentina's heartland, spreads over an area of about 250,000 square miles, 23 per cent of the nation. The Pampa was once the bed of an inland sea, and its deep alluvial soil is **extremely fertile**—perfect for wheat, corn and grazing grass.

PRIMITIVE OXCARTS with outsized wheels haul logs out of a junglelike region of the Gran Chaco in Paraguay. The Gran Chaco is a low-lying, subtropical plain of dense scrub forest and grassland which covers much of Paraguay and stretches into northern Argentina. In winter it is parched; in the summer it is flooded and temperatures reach as high as

115° F. But for all the difficulties that the Chaco presents, it is Paraguay's chief cattle-raising area and yields valuable quebracho wood, which contains a high percentage of tannin, a chemical used in tanning leather. The wood itself is extremely durable (quebracho means "ax breaker") and is ideal for railroad ties and bridge construction. Some logs weigh five tons.

WIND-BLOWN LAKE named Nahuel Huapí is in the mountainous Bariloche area of western Argentina, which resembles Switzerland. The region was, in fact, settled by Swiss immigrants.

LUSH PASTURE near Lake Nahuel Huapí has a golden fringe of poplars which, like many Argentine trees, were imported from Europe. In the background rises the great Andean wall.

BARREN HILLS near Bariloche look down on a Gaucho herdsman as he rides beside one of the area's many mountain streams. Bariloche is best known as a smart international resort, with winter skiing on nearby Andean slopes and fishing in the summer. Fishing is so recent a development that many of the streams do not yet have names and are designated by number.

2

The Natives
and the
Newcomers

THE River Plate area today is predominantly European in descent and culture. Of Argentina's 22 million people, more than 90 per cent are white; among Uruguay's 2.6 millions the percentage is about the same; only in Paraguay is there a mestizo, or mixed Spanish-Indian, majority, but even there the national culture is basically European.

As in North America, however, these were not empty lands when the first white men arrived in the 16th Century. The area was already inhabited, and by the same peoples as North America, all of whom were erroneously known as *indios*, or Indians, as a result of Columbus' mistaken belief that he had reached Asia. In only two parts of the Americas had these Indians achieved a high degree of civilization: in Mexico and Central America, which saw the bloodthirsty but otherwise sophisticated cultures of the Aztecs and their predecessors, the Maya; and in the Andean highlands, where the Inca developed what a French writer has called their "socialist empire." This Inca Empire at the time of the Spanish conquest stretched from what is now Colombia to a point some distance within the borders of present-day Chile and Argentina. Even today in the northern Argentine Provinces of Jujuy and Salta, the old Inca language, Quechua, is still spoken in a debased form, as it is in much of neighboring Bolivia and throughout the Peruvian highlands. Of the other River Plate Indians, only one group, the Guarani, had achieved any kind of settled, organized existence before the white man came; and their empire stretched across large areas of present-day Uruguay, southern Brazil, the Argentine Provinces of Corrientes and Misiones, and Paraguay east of the Chaco.

In Paraguay, where almost everybody is of part-Guarani descent, school textbooks devote considerable space to descriptions of the Guarani at the time of the conquest. They are portrayed as being of medium height and compact build, with broad hips, well-developed muscles, small hands and feet, and little facial hair. Modern Paraguayans are also taught that their ancestors were reserved in manner, with a great command of their emotions. Their expression was enigmatic, they spoke seldom, and they bore suffering stoically. Their senses were acute and their perceptions rapid. The modern pure-bred Guarani still has these characteristics.

The ancient Guarani had a neolithic type of culture based on the cultivation of the soil; hunting and fishing were secondary activities. Their agricultural methods were comparatively advanced, and they lived in large communal houses made of tree trunks and leaves which housed whole family groups. Early Spanish chroniclers reported with horror that the Guarani were cannibals. So, evidently, they were, but this custom, deeply rooted in the magical beliefs of the tribe, was not practiced indiscriminately, being solely confined to the ritual consumption of prisoners of war.

PRIMITIVE though the Guarani may have been, they were relatively peaceful and more capable of coping with the arrival of bearded white strangers from overseas than were the remaining Indian tribes, such as the Charrua and Chana of Uruguay, the Araucanians and Querendi of Argentina, and the Ona and Alcaluf of Tierra del Fuego. Unlike the Guarani, these peoples lived almost exclusively by hunting and fishing and were entirely nomadic. They had a good deal in common with the Indians of North America, including a determination to resist the white man's encroachments.

Despite their backwardness, the Indians had a familiarity with their own land and an ability to live off the country, which gave them an advantage over the cumbrously equipped Spaniards, often weakened and sick after a long journey across the ocean. The Spaniards had none of the technical advantages of modern colonizers, and however appalling their methods may seem today, their courage was extraordinary. As an Argentine writer has put it: "The conquest of America was made with blood and fire; . . . it was the work of civilized barbarism struggling with the barbarism of the jungle."

THE first European to discover the River Plate was Juan Díaz de Solís, who arrived in the wide estuary in February 1516, after a voyage of four months from Spain. With a few companions, he disembarked on the coast of Uruguay, probably near the present-day resort of Punta del Este, and with magnificent effrontery "took possession" of the whole region in the name of the Spanish Crown. Soon thereafter, most historians agree, he and his party were attacked by a band of warlike Charrua Indians. De Solís was killed, together with all but one of his companions, who, badly wounded, was nursed back to health, perhaps by a group of peaceful Guarani. A decade later, this survivor, Francisco del Puerto, was found by another Spanish expedition for which, so legend has it, he was able to serve as interpreter. If this tale is true, Del Puerto was the first Spaniard to speak Guarani, now the only flourishing indigenous language of the River Plate area.

The second major expedition to the River Plate was almost as disastrous as the first. Led by Don Pedro de Mendoza, it arrived in February 1536 and founded the settlement of Nuestra Señora Santa María del Buen Aire, or Our Lady Holy Mary of the Fair Wind, today Buenos Aires. The settlement at first was little more than a primitive, fortified village constructed of the inadequate materials at hand, but the Spaniards liked to give grandiloquent names to the most unpromising places.

The region was at the time occupied by the Querendi, and after a short period of peaceful coexistence, the settlers found themselves surrounded by 23,000 hostile Indians. The Spaniards held out for some five years in the face of hunger and frequent attacks, but eventually the settlement was abandoned. It was not refounded until 1580, when Juan de Garay came downriver with a group of settlers from already established Asunción and, as if to give the settlement permanent reality with an even longer title, renamed it Ciudad de la Santísima Trinidad y Puerto de Santa María de Buenos Aires. Asunción itself, which for many years was the political headquarters of the entire River Plate region, had been founded 43 years before, in 1537.

Of the 63 companions whom Garay brought with him, only 11 were Spaniards born in Spain itself. The other 52 were "Spanish Americans," which in contemporary usage meant that they had been born in South America of Spanish fathers and Indian mothers. This was significant: in subsequent years, it was not only warfare that caused the virtual disappearance of identifiable "natives." More "colonial" Argentine families have some Indian blood than would care to admit it.

Unlike the Anglo-Saxon settlers in North America, the Spaniards regarded their mestizo, or mixed blood, progeny as European rather than Indian, and these people so regarded themselves. Writing in 1612, in a book entitled *La Argentina*, the Asunción-born mestizo Ruy Díaz de Guzmán showed the same attitude toward his purely aboriginal contemporaries as the most diehard white settler. He characterized the Querendi and other Indians as treacherous and bloody villains, "the mortal enemies of the Spaniards."

While European settlement from the Atlantic proceeded slowly and bloodily, it began to be mightily reinforced from the northwest. Expeditions from the well-established Spanish communities in Peru and Chile were already crossing the Andes, and between 1553 and 1596 the cities of Santiago del Estero, Tucumán (on the site of a former Inca settlement), Córdoba, Salta, La Rioja, Jujuy, Mendoza, San Juan and San Luis—all of them today the capitals of

Argentine provinces—were founded. Throughout the 17th and 18th Centuries, the Spanish population grew slowly and the number of Indians continued to dwindle, though it was not until 1879 to 1883, in the "Conquest of the Desert," led by the Argentine General Julio A. Roca, that the Indians were finally subdued and large numbers of them were killed.

But before this dubious victory was achieved, miscegenation between Spaniard and Indian had produced an almost separate breed of people, the Gauchos, who were to play a great part in River Plate history and a greater one in legend, and who have become a national symbol of both Argentina and Uruguay.

The Gauchos belonged to the desolate expanse of the Pampa, just as the cowboys did to the Western plains of the U.S. Their life was conditioned by the existence of the huge herds of cattle and half-wild horses that roamed over the unfenced Pampa. They were often attacked by raiding Indians, and they held life cheap—both their own and other people's. They had few wants that their horses and cattle could not satisfy. "Vain is the endeavour to explain to him [the Gaucho] the luxuries and blessings of a more civilized life," an English traveler wrote in 1826; "his ideas are, that the noblest effort of man is to raise himself off the ground and ride instead of walk—that no rich garments or variety of food can atone for the want of a horse—and that the print of the human foot on the ground is in his mind the symbol of uncivilization."

The Gauchos slept under the open sky, with a saddle for a pillow. On their feet they wore *botas de potro* (literally, filly boots) made of hide stripped from a colt's hind leg and pulled on while still moist, so that the boots fitted the owner as if

A RIVER PLATE GLOSSARY

A number of terms used in the River Plate countries—and in this volume—are explained in the following brief glossary.

Porteños, or port dwellers, is a word that describes the residents of Buenos Aires.

Rioplatenses is a name given the peoples who live on the banks of the River Plate, and by extension to all citizens of the three River Plate nations.

Estancieros are the owners of vast ranches, or *estancias*.

Orientales is an old, but still current, term for the citizens of Uruguay, who live on the Banda Oriental, or eastern bank, of the Uruguay River.

Creole (Criollo) is a term denoting anyone of Spanish parentage born in the Americas.

Mestizo is the Spanish word for people of mixed European and Indian ancestry.

Reducciones were the Indian villages set up by the Jesuits in the 17th Century to convert the Indian population of the River Plate.

custom-tailored. There was an aperture for the big toe to facilitate control of the horse, this free toe gripping the crude stirrups, which often consisted merely of a bone attached to a leather thong.

The Gauchos, like many modern Argentines, considered the word "food" to be synonymous with "meat." All their sports were on horseback. If they possessed a dwelling at all, it was a simple shack, its privacy preserved only by a cowhide drape. Their only article of cutlery was an all-purpose knife. One of the many 19th Century British travelers who were fascinated by the romance of the Gaucho wrote in 1853: "The use of a fork is avoided, because a knife and fork require a plate, which needs to be placed on a table. This want creates another: a table involves the necessity of a chair; and thus the consequences resulting from the use of forks involves a complete revolution in the household."

T HE Gaucho way of life existed well into the late 19th Century, and indeed into the beginning of the 20th. The Gauchos inspired Ricardo Güiraldes' prose epic *Don Segundo Sombra* and José Hernández' Creole verse epic *Martín Fierro*, parts of which, like parts of Shakespeare and the King James Bible in English-speaking countries, have passed into current colloquial speech.

But today the unfenced fields have been fenced, and the descendant of the free-riding Gaucho is likely to be a paid worker on an *estancia*, perhaps still riding a horse but more likely driving a tractor or a combine. He lives in a house with a wife and family, collects a salary and goes into the nearest town on weekends to dance, not the old *escondido* or even the comparatively modern tango, which he generally sits out, but whatever dance is currently "in" from Boston to Bangkok.

He may, with almost equal likelihood, be a gas-station attendant on Argentina's National Highway No. 1 or an assembly-line worker in a Córdoba automobile factory. Whatever he does, he will certainly have a radio and probably a television set. Culturally, if not entirely racially, the victory of European customs and manners and patterns of life in the River Plate has been virtually complete.

In most Latin American countries, there has been a third factor in the human situation: the African.

The effect of Negro culture on Brazil, for instance, has been great—in customs, language and even religion. In other Latin American countries, there are African minorities which have had an effect on their national cultures, but these countries do not include the River Plate republics.

Yet African slaves *were* brought into the River Plate area during the 17th and 18th Centuries, and though they left no mark in Paraguay, they played a considerable part in the development of Argentina and Uruguay. Old prints portray Negroes as house servants, coachmen and gardeners. As late as the 1880s, according to an English encyclopedia, "In Buenos Ayres and about the shores of La Plata negro slaves were formerly numerous, and their progeny are still distinguishable among the colored population."

In Argentina they are not distinguishable any more; in the whole country, there are probably not more than a few thousand recognized Negroes. The rest have been totally assimilated through intermarriage. It is possible to spend a lifetime in Buenos Aires without meeting a single Negro, except a sailor off a foreign ship.

I N Uruguay, both in the city of Montevideo and out in what Anglo-Platenses call in English "the camp"—from the Spanish *el campo*, "the interior"—one still finds Negroes. They are particularly noticeable in the Army. The reason is reputed to be that when slavery was finally abolished in neighboring Brazil in 1888, many of the former slaves moved south to Uruguay, to leave the land where they had endured servitude. Upon arrival, they realized that they were inexperienced in finding houses, signing contracts and in general exercising their rights as free men; so they joined the Uruguayan Army, where, although free, they enjoyed the security of a regimented, orderly life.

The surviving Negroes in Uruguay are not discriminated against. Civil rights legislation, such as that which the U.S. enacted in 1964, would benefit them nothing since they are already free to frequent any café, bar, movie theater or beach and can use any means of public transport; they can send their children to any school they choose, attend any church they like and vote in any election. Yet, in a country that justifiably claims to have no proletariat, most Negroes belong to the class just above it, the lower middle. There are few, if any, Negroes in the ranks of businessmen or university professors. However, it is fair to say that, despite this silent, submerged discrimination, there are no black ghettos preyed upon by piratical slumlords.

WHILE the Africans, in number and influence, have had little lasting effect on the River Plate region, people from other European countries besides Spain most definitely have. Among the European residents and settlers, the British have played a particularly influential part, becoming indeed almost a part of the landscape, so that writers like the Argentine-born W. H. Hudson and the Scottish Robert Cunninghame Graham (known throughout the River Plate as Don Roberto) were and still are regarded by Rioplatenses as compatriots.

This was natural, since these writers, and many other Britons, identified themselves with the River Plate nations and felt a strong attachment to the people. In fact, except for the more numerous immigrants from Spain and Italy, the main and most lasting contribution to River Plate trade and to the area's social and political growth has come from the British, the majority of whom settled in Argentina.

There were already a number of British merchants in Buenos Aires at the end of the period of Spanish rule, but it was during the 19th Century that they began to make their imprint felt. The first trickles of English immigration were enthusiastically encouraged in 1826 by His Britannic Majesty's Minister to the United Provinces of the River Plate, Lord Ponsonby. He wrote: "The Settler finds here an abundance of Horses and Cattle, a rich soil, and a constant and easy communication with England: Religion [i.e., Protestantism] not only tolerated but respected; and persons and property as well protected as the persons and property of the native inhabitants, and a prospect, almost a certainty, that by industry and skill a considerable fortune may be rapidly accumulated."

Whether or not they were aware of Ponsonby's views, the British from the 1820s on started to come in significant numbers to Argentina and in smaller numbers to Uruguay. Following the merchants

came ranchers who bought large tracts of land from the Argentine Government for minimal prices and subsequently, as Ponsonby predicted, became rich. Following the ranchers came the administrators and technicians employed by the railroads, gasworks and other utilities which British firms and capital were building in Argentina and Uruguay. Since the climate was temperate and the inhabitants civilized, the British tended to settle permanently, as in Canada or Australia, rather than to return home to retire, as from Africa or India. By the middle of the 19th Century, the Anglo-Argentine community numbered in the thousands, and in 1871 the British consul reported that there were 10,533 British subjects in Buenos Aires—and this, of course, did not include the few people of British descent who had taken Argentine nationality.

Although the British-owned railroads have now been nationalized, as have the Anglo-Argentine Tramways Company, the British-owned gasworks and similar enterprises, the British influence in Argentina remains strong and has considerably affected Argentine life. The British contribution was characterized by President Bartolomé Mitre as "the principal factor in the country's political, social and economic progress."

THE Anglo-Argentine community, whose members are invariably bilingual, is still numbered in the thousands—some estimates are as high as 70,000—and its influence is still apparent. The names of the Buenos Aires suburbs of Banfield, Temperley, Hurlingham and Ranelagh give evidence of their origin. Many Argentines of the upper classes send their sons to Roman Catholic "public" (i.e., private preparatory) schools in Britain, such as Beaumont College, Ampleforth and Stonyhurst, and then on to Oxford. Afternoon tea is a normal Argentine middle-class custom. One of the biggest stores in Buenos Aires is Harrods, counterpart of its original in London, while the downtown section of the city has solid, Edwardian-looking pubs called the Alexandra, the London Grill and Lloyd's Bar. It is possible to spend a lifetime in Buenos Aires without speaking a word of anything but English.

Among the United Kingdom immigrants, the Welsh form a special community. In 1863, when the

Welsh in Wales were chafing under what they regarded as English religious and cultural domination, the Welsh Emigration Society signed a contract with the Argentine Government undertaking to establish colonies in Patagonia at the rate of 300 to 500 families annually for 10 years. But the Welsh on arrival showed no more amenability to Argentine hegemony than they had to English. They had emigrated from Wales with the purpose of preserving their own language and customs, so they kept to themselves and continued to speak Welsh.

In the early 1900s an Argentine educational inspection revealed that children in the state schools in Trelew, Patagonia, even if they were named Rodríguez rather than Williams, were being taught Welsh language and literature at the Argentine taxpayers' expense. The Welsh were also resisting conscription into the Argentine Army and especially military drill on Sunday. In their efforts to avoid becoming Argentines, the Welsh appealed for support to the British Legation in Buenos Aires. The British Minister replied that since the complainants had renounced British citizenship he could do nothing. Subsequently the British Government did help a number of the Welsh re-emigrate to Canada. But most stayed—and today the sermons in the austere Protestant chapels in the Welsh villages of Patagonia are still delivered in Welsh.

THE Irish, as Catholics, settled in more easily. Many went out to Argentina as construction workers on the railroads in the late 19th Century, married local girls and became Argentines in one generation. Others went as simple shepherds, bought hundreds of square miles of sheep-grazing land for virtually nothing and rapidly became rich, so that today names like O'Farrell appear regularly in the Buenos Aires society magazines.

Of the other northern European peoples, the Germans have made the most impact on the River Plate, and on Argentina in particular, though there are families of German origin in Uruguay and the father of President Alfredo Stroessner of Paraguay was German. Some of the Germans proved to be undesirable settlers: in 1884, for instance, the leader of an anti-Semitic movement, one Dr. Forster, led a migration to Argentina, and people of a similar cast

of mind arrived both before and after World War II. But most of the early German immigrants were Social Democrats, and the German-language daily, the *Argentinisches Tageblatt,* is proud of the fact that it was apparently the first overseas newspaper to be banned by Hitler in 1933.

The German immigrants, like the British, tended to be middle class. The same is true of the Dutch and the Scandinavians. The bulk of working-class immigration from the mid-19th Century onward came from the Mediterranean countries, notably Spain and Italy. The official census of 1895 gave Argentina's total population as 3,954,811, of whom 1,005,427 were foreign-born; and between 1857 and 1910, the peak immigration years, the net total of arrivals from overseas was about 2,260,000. Of these, some 80 per cent came from Spain or Italy.

CURIOUSLY enough the Spaniards, many of them illiterate peasants, were the slower of the two groups to become integrated. A large proportion came from the backward region of Galicia, unlike the "colonial" Argentines, who had come mostly from Andalusia, and to this day the more recent Spanish immigrants are generically known as *gallegos,* or Galicians, wherever they have come from. They tend to do menial jobs, becoming grocery clerks, bartenders, waiters, taxi drivers and doormen.

The Italians, in contrast, keep to no such narrow occupational limitations. They have provided Argentina with everything from unskilled laborers to presidents; they have settled in both the cities and "the camp"; they have provided the Argentine-Spanish language with so many imported words that many Argentines can converse quite comfortably in southern Italy and laugh at the jokes in undubbed Italian films. The Italians have proliferated to such an extent that 40 per cent of all Argentines have Italian blood, and the Buenos Aires telephone directory lists more Italian surnames than Spanish.

The Jews came to Argentina principally in three waves, the first and last of them caused by persecution abroad. The first group, known colloquially as *Rusos,* was brought to Argentina in the 1890s from Russia by the German-Jewish financier and philanthropist Baron Maurice de Hirsch. They settled in Santa Fe and Entre Ríos, though some of them later moved to the capital. They were mostly of lower-class origin. The second group of Jews, most of whom arrived in the 1920s, came not to avoid persecution but simply to find a better life. The third group, almost entirely middle class, arrived in the 1930s as refugees from Nazi persecution.

The same is roughly true of the Jewish community in Uruguay. That country's recent pattern of immigration is similar to Argentina's, though on a much smaller scale, and the Spanish strain is still far more predominant. And the people who have settled in Uruguay have become more swiftly assimilated, perhaps because it is a smaller country.

Paraguay, because of its comparative remoteness, its difficult terrain and its turbulent history, has had less happy experiences with its immigrants. The first of many disastrous ventures took place in 1872. Part of a Paraguayan loan raised in London was set aside to finance a settlement of "Lincolnshire Farmers" near Asunción. The contractors collected, instead of Lincolnshire farmers, 800 "needy artisans from the streets of London" and sent them to a rural part of Paraguay where no arrangements had been made to house or feed them. In six months 162 of them died from exposure and undernourishment, and the remainder gave up and re-emigrated to Argentina.

IN 1893 a new emigration scheme was launched from, of all places, Australia. Of the fate of these immigrants the British author George Pendle writes: "The settlers surrendered all their possessions to the common fund of the [New Australian Co-operative Settlement] Association; they pledged themselves to teetotalism 'until the initial difficulties of settlement have passed'; and a first contingent of 250 emigrants embarked at Sydney in a small sailing ship, the *Royal Tar*. Arrived at Villarica, they set to work building adobe huts and fencing their pastures for cattle.

"Dissension soon developed, however, several of the colonists having broken their pledge of abstinence by drinking 'Paraguayan rum' *(caña)*. These men were expelled from the colony . . . and were joined by a number of voluntary seceders. There were grievances and intrigues, and the women 'gave trouble,' some husbands complaining that 'while

perfectly contented with their day's work they were positively afraid to face the nocturnal music in their connubial tents.'"

In 1894 a second group arrived from Adelaide with more success. They abandoned the cooperative system and acquired land of their own, and many of them did well. On the whole, however, immigration to Paraguay remained a mere trickle: between 1905 and 1925, when the arrivals in the seaboard River Plate countries amounted to hundreds of thousands, the total immigration to Paraguay was 13,258—mostly Germans, Spaniards and Italians. One of the most successful groups since then has been the Mennonites, who began to arrive from Canada in 1927. Economically they have benefited the land of their adoption, although culturally and socially they have kept aloof —as the members of this strict religious sect usually tend to do.

Thus Paraguay has remained basically Spanish and Guarani, while Argentina and Uruguay have become polyglot and cosmopolitan. But just as in the United States a similar phenomenon has produced a nostalgia for the Old West and the open frontier, so in Argentina and Uruguay growing cosmopolitanism has given rise to a cult of the vanished Gaucho and of everything Creole. Suburban, commuting Buenos Aires families, whose forefathers liked to ape everything European, ostentatiously drink maté (Paraguayan tea) from gourds through silver tubes and use rural colloquialisms which their ancestors would have disdained. The stately Buenos Aires daily *La Prensa* in 1964 started a Gaucho comic strip, "Fabián Leyes," whose characters' dialogue makes Texan sound like the purest academic English.

THIS mystique was notably encouraged during Perón's highly nationalistic dictatorship and before that by the Argentine interim military governments of 1943 to 1945, whose members were perpetually stressing everything that was "Creole" or "100 per cent Argentine." Only a few cynics drew attention to the fact that these 100 per cent Argentines included President Farrell, Foreign Minister Gilbert (pronounced as in French), Minister of Agriculture Mason, Presidential Secretary Tauber and Chief of Staff General von der Becke. The contents of the melting pot had melted.

WEARING A MANTILLA, a young girl emerges from a church in Córdoba, Argentina. For upper-class Argentine girls, social life is carefully supervised, as it is in southern Europe.

Masters of the Art of Good Living

For city-dwelling Argentines and Uruguayans, leisure is an art. They love large, lengthy meals. Good manners and careful—even dapper—dressing are all-important. Small pleasures are savored: an evening stroll, an hour over coffee, a day in the sun. Ethnically and in their traditions, Argentina and Uruguay are the most "European" nations in Latin America. But sometimes a New World flair for competition prevails over the people's studied urbanity, and they become aggressive and ferocious sports fans.

SIPPING COFFEE, the patrons of a sidewalk café pass a relaxed Sunday afternoon in Buenos Aires. The city is full of these open-air spots, as well as quiet tearooms and espresso bars.

BUYING FLOWERS, a Buenos Aires businessman (opposite) pauses on his way home from the office. The numerous streetside flower stalls give the rather drab city a more sprightly air.

golden beaches and leisured living

MODERN BEACH HOUSE fronting on the sea *(above)* suggests the informal but luxurious atmosphere of Punta del Este. Many of "Punta's" lavish villas are hidden away in pine groves.

SUN-DRENCHED CAFE not far from the surf *(left)* provides vacationers a place to talk, drink and get a tan. In the background, hotels line one of Punta del Este's curving beaches.

EXPENSIVE AUTOMOBILE pulls up *(below)* beside a house opposite a crowded yacht basin. Punta del Este has two shores: one facing the sheltered River Plate, the other the Atlantic.

35

HUGE VACATION SPOT in Argentina,
Mar del Plata welcomes more than
a million people every summer

A crowd packs the beach in front of Mar del Plata's casino

Sightseers at Mar del Plata descend from a fancifully decorated

FOLDED UMBRELLAS give the beach *(left)* a doleful look on a cloudy day. In the background looms the casino, which draws up to 20,000 customers a night.

The resort has 1,200 hotels and boardinghouses for its visitors.

bus. A highway connected the resort with Buenos Aires in 1939.

SEA OF CANVAS virtually hides the sand *(right)* on the ocean front. A mass invasion of the resort comes in December, when workers get an obligatory year-end bonus.

FINISHING A ROUND, golfers putt out on the 18th green of the golf course in Palermo Park *(above)*. Largest and most popular of Buenos Aires' recreation areas, Palermo includes a race track, tennis courts, riding trails, a polo field and numerous athletic clubs. Less strenuous citizens go there to cook beefsteaks on portable stoves or just to take a nap in the shade.

RIDING A STATUE commemorating beef, Argentina's best-known export *(above)*, children play in Buenos Aires' resort suburb of Tigre, famous for its flowers and rare tropical plants.

ROWING BOATS, a popular pastime around Tigre, requires considerable skill, since the surrounding area, part of the delta of the Paraná River, is a wilderness of intricate channels.

DIGNIFIED PATRONS of a quiet, paneled *confitería*, or pastry shop *(above)*, idle at teatime. To have a snack at a *confitería* at dusk is an established Buenos Aires habit. The *confiterías* serve sandwiches and cocktails as well as tea and pastries.

MIDDAY SHOPPERS crowd Calle Florida *(left)*, which boasts some of Buenos Aires' best jewelers and leather goods shops. At 6 o'clock the street becomes the scene of the evening *paseo*, or walk, when people stroll about just to look at one another.

HURRIED CLERKS chalk up stock quotations *(opposite)* as traders fill the floor of the Bolsa, the Buenos Aires stock exchange. Traditionally the scene of wild speculations, the Bolsa has begun to attract smaller and more conservative investors.

*BUSY CITY of
Buenos Aires thrives
on hard work and a
grueling round
of entertainments*

WHITE-COATED WAITER serves customers at a restaurant *(right)* specializing in a Gaucho-style barbecue called *asado (foreground)*. The meat is barbecued vertically over a roaring wood fire and is basted with fat running down its length.

SPORTING EVENTS draw huge crowds in Buenos Aires as the people indulge their love of competition

MASSED FANS watch a soccer match *(left)* between two Buenos Aires clubs. Soccer is virtually a religion, and the city has 23 stadiums, often drawing a million spectators on a single day.

AVID BETTORS study their racing sheets with anguished concentration at the Palermo track *(opposite)*. Palermo is the site of Argentina's most important race, the Gran Premio Nacional.

JITTERY RACE HORSES parade before racing buffs in the paddock of the Palermo track *(below)*. Palermo's stands hold 45,000 people and are jammed every day of the three-month season.

During a Uruguayan festival, Creole Week, held in Montevideo, one man in traditional Gaucho attire flirts with an unresponsive girl a

another assumes the Gaucho's favorite pose—sitting on horseback.

3

Neglected Outposts of a Great Empire

NORTH AMERICAN and British editorial writers and speechmakers often link Latin America with Asia and Africa when referring to the needs or problems of the "developing" countries or ex-colonial territories.

This is misleading, for although Latin America as a whole is largely underdeveloped and ex-colonial, it is (like the United States) basically European in culture, language and religion. In the case of the River Plate countries, the population is also, as we have seen, predominantly of European stock. Yet there is *some* truth in the grouping together of Latin America with Asia and Africa. The opposition of the Latin American republics, including those of the River Plate, to "colonialism," their reluctance to be seriously involved in the East-West struggle, their touchy insistence on national sovereignty—all these they share with the Africans and Asians.

Leaving aside the economic causes, this attitude has a historical basis. The past 150 years of independence were preceded by nearly 300 under colonial rule; and colonists from Europe can be just as irked by their "home" governments as Africans and Asians can by their colonial overlords. The vandals who perpetrated the Boston Tea Party were dressed up like Indians, but they were, in fact, men of British stock and subjects of the Crown.

In the River Plate, this annoyance was exacerbated by the colonists being treated as "poor relations" in the Spanish Empire. Nowadays, when the River Plate basin is one of the richest agricultural and pastoral areas of the world, this may seem paradoxical. But the Spanish conquistadors were not interested in settling as farmers, nor was the Spanish Government interested at first in their doing so. Even less did the Government wish to promote an export trade that would compete with Spanish products. What both the conquistadors and the Spanish Government *were* interested in were gold and silver. In the words of the Paraguayan historian Julio César Chaves, they suffered from *"la ilusión de las grandes riquezas"* (the illusion of great riches). Indeed, they hoped that the wealth of El Dorado—the fabled Golden City of the Americas—might be found in the River Plate region. It was this hope that caused the muddy estuary to be given its inappropriate name.

THE new world which the conquistadors opened up was seen simply as a means of enriching Spain, or rather the Spanish Crown. In the words of Professor J. Fred Rippy, a U.S. expert on Latin American history: "That this New World belonged to the Spanish monarchs and not to the Spanish nation was fundamental. They successfully asserted not only their sovereign rights in America but their property rights as well. Every privilege, office, and position, whether political, administrative, judicial, economic, or religious, must come from them. It was from this basis that the exploration, conquest, occupation, and government of the New World proceeded."

In Spain itself the supreme authority, under the monarch, was the Royal and Supreme Council of the Indies. The council was organized as an independent body in 1524—only 32 years after Columbus had first cast eyes on the new continent. The council's powers covered all aspects of colonial administration: it employed chroniclers and cosmographers, prepared all the laws and statutes submitted for royal approval, and chose and supervised the officials who were sent to the Americas. It was also the supreme court of appeal for all sentences passed in the colonies. After almost 200 years of rule, it was shorn of its powers in 1714, but the colonists noticed little difference, as many of its former functions were taken over by the Cabinet minister in charge of the Office of the Indies.

Many of the first Spanish authorities to function on American soil were given the title of *adelantado* (literally, one who goes on ahead). These men had rights of apportioning land and labor and had full political, administrative and military powers in the areas under their jurisdiction. But the *adelantados* soon grew too independent and powerful to be controlled by the distant home Government, and by the end of the 16th Century they had been replaced by a complicated colonial hierarchy, formed at all the top levels by Spanish-born officials and responsible only to the Crown.

At the peak of the hierarchic pyramid in America stood the viceroys, with powers second only to the distant king himself. It is symptomatic of the lack of prestige of the River Plate area in Spanish minds that until 1776 it came under the Viceroyalty of Peru, which was centered in the opulent court at Lima, and Buenos Aires for many years had to receive its instructions from Lima by way of an intermediary headquarters in Asunción.

Next in authority to the viceroys came the governors and captains-general, who held sway over areas such as present-day Paraguay, Uruguay and the larger Argentine provinces. Since these men were mostly soldiers, often barely literate and ignorant in matters of civil government, they were usually assisted in the exercise of their functions by an *asesor letrado,* or learned adviser, known colloquially as an *hombre de toga* from the togalike garment worn by academics.

THE only "grassroots" political authorities were the *cabildos,* or municipal councils. These bodies, copied from the *municipios,* or town governments, of Spain, were only in the most restricted sense democratic, since all their members had to be citizens, which then meant men who owned a significant amount of property. The ordinary inhabitants, such as Indians, mestizos and Negroes, played no part in them. The *cabildos* were important, however, since they were the only political bodies in which Creoles were represented and were virtually the only bodies through which local people could have a voice in the management of their own affairs.

Many of the big estates were run on the encomienda system. This system, although this was not its original purpose, made the Spanish settlers, in effect, feudal overlords. The Spanish Crown, on the advice of eminent jurists, had decreed that the Indians of the Americas were free men and not, as many of the Spanish colonists insisted, slaves. But since the economic development of the continent required manual labor, which the Spaniards would not stoop to and the Indians were loath to supply, a halfway system was introduced by which the Indians were obliged to work for the Spaniard to whom they were assigned, while he in turn had certain obligations toward them, seeing to their welfare and instructing them in the Christian faith.

ALTHOUGH the Crown's laws governing encomiendas were meant to be uniformly applied, in practice the development of the system varied in different areas of the New World. Land grants given by the Spanish Government to its colonists sometimes included the labor of resident Indians. More often the two grants were separate. In Paraguay, for instance, some encomienda Indians lived in villages on their own land and were periodically brought in to cultivate the encomienda holder's fields; others lived in villages on the property of the landowner; and still others lived as servants in the households of landowners.

But while the Indian could not avoid providing the labor, the landholder did not always live up to his duty of caring for and Christianizing his charges. Again, conditions varied from place to place. The rigid Spanish laws designed to protect the Indians and restrict their labor were more easily disregarded in outlying Paraguay than in places like the West Indies. On the other hand, in Paraguay the early unions of Spaniards and Guarani women, which resulted in a racially mixed population, together with the poverty of the Paraguayan economy, combined to make the interests of Indian and Spaniard more compatible than was the case in other areas of Spanish colonization. The anthropologist Elman R. Service puts it this way: "The Spaniards in Paraguay were, truly enough, the exploiters, and the Indians were exploited, but as this occurred within a subsistence economy, it was a situation at least comprehensible to the Indians, and probably even a more acceptable one than it might have been under the conditions of a commercial economy."

THE Christianizing of Indians was more determinedly carried out by the Church's own apostles in the New World, who also laid claim to large tracts of land. In fact, the secular colonists as well as the Crown relied heavily on the religious orders to pacify the Indians and make them docile workers. This is not to say, however, that the Roman Catholic Church in the Americas was merely a hypocritical arm of the secular colonizing power. There were undoubtedly a number of clergy who failed to live up to their high calling, but this was not the general rule, and many priests did much to mitigate the lot of the Indians and restrain the cruelty of the settlers —for instance, Fray Bartolomé de Las Casas (1474-1566), who for many years indefatigably represented the interests of the Indians at the Spanish court.

The task both of the priests and of the conscientious laymen, official and unofficial, who supported their efforts was difficult, often thankless and sometimes dangerous. An early Governor of the River Plate (and the first Creole Governor in the area) was Hernando Arias de Saavedra, more commonly known as Hernandarias. After fruitless attempts to subdue the Indians, who then greatly outnumbered the Spaniards, Hernandarias came to the enlightened conclusion that the only possible solution was a peaceful one, and the only way of achieving it was to convert the Indians to Christianity (although a look at contemporary Christian Europe, wracked by religious wars, would not have given much encouragement to this thesis).

His successor, Diego de Góngora, taking office in 1618, decided to put Hernandarias' theories into practice. The preaching, historians report, did not result in many conversions, but some of the Indian chiefs went to Buenos Aires and were entertained by Governor Góngora and his successor, Don Francisco de Céspedes. Céspedes encouraged trade with the Indians, lavished attentions and gifts on them, received them in small groups in Buenos Aires and achieved a measure of mutual understanding in the face of Indian suspicion. In this work he enlisted the aid of the Franciscans and Jesuits. The Charrua and the Yaro put up no resistance to the peaceful passage of the priests through their country, but the greatest triumph was obtained with the Chana, who, abandoning their scattered settlement on the islands of the lower Río Negro, came together in about 1624 to found Santo Domingo de Soriano, the oldest organized settlement in Uruguay. Other *reducciones,* or missionary settlements, were built in the same area, although no trace remains of them today.

These *reducciones* were populated by Christianized Chana and Yaro, and also by white and mestizo Paraguayans brought by the missionaries to help the process of adaptation. But the indoctrination of another tribe of Indians, the Charrua, proved impossible. "The rebellious character of these people," according to the Uruguayan historians Schurmann and Coolighan, "would not tolerate either the circumscribed life or the discipline characteristic of evangelical missions, and the Charrua in a very short time became the implacable and tenacious enemies of these social nuclei."

But however difficult the task of conversion might be, the Spaniards, both clerical and lay, had been commanded to persevere in it by no less an authority than the Pope. In 1493, as soon as news of the New World discoveries reached Europe, Spain's Ferdinand and Isabella—fearing Portuguese competition—took their claim to the land Columbus had discovered to Pope Alexander VI for confirmation. The Pope (who was a Spaniard) obligingly replied with a series of bulls granting to Spain all lands west of a north-south line drawn 100 leagues beyond the Cape Verde Islands (off Africa's Atlantic coast). Portugal was

dissatisfied with the Pope's generosity toward Spain, and King John of Portugal opened negotiations with the Spanish monarchs. Both countries, wishing at that moment to avoid open conflict, finally agreed —in the 1494 Treaty of Tordesillas—to move the line marking the Spanish claim farther westward. This new line turned out to run through the middle of modern-day Brazil—as the result of which Brazil today speaks Portuguese and all the rest of Latin America speaks Spanish.

While the papal line of demarcation was changed, the Pope's instructions that the colonizers must Christianize the natives remained in force. In the religious climate of the 15th Century, it was a command that no Christian nation, let alone Spain or Portugal, would have dared to disobey.

Theoretically the secular and the religious pioneers worked in harmony for the same ideal. In fact, friction quickly developed between them. The religious orders founded their establishments in the no man's land between the Spanish-settled areas and Indian territory. Inevitably, as the missionaries advanced toward the forests, the white colonists tried to move into the territory already settled by the missions.

In the River Plate the most important religious order was that of the Jesuits, who concentrated principally on Paraguay, founding the headquarters of their first American Provincia Jesuítica there in 1607. This was followed in 1610 by the mission of San Ignacio Guazú (*guazú*—or *guasú*—is the Guarani word for "great") and by several *reducciones*.

The early Jesuit missions have been described as fundamentally communist. Although they would not qualify under any current definition of Marxism-Leninism, they would fulfill the definition of communism in the *Concise Oxford Dictionary:* "Vesting of property in the community, each member working according to his capacity and receiving according

---

THE PIONEERING JESUIT ORDER

The Jesuits, or members of the Society of Jesus, were among the conquerors of the Paraguayan and Uruguayan wilderness. The Society was founded in 1540 by Saint Ignatius Loyola to help stem the tide of the Reformation. Energetic missionaries, the Jesuits since that time have devoted themselves to spreading Christianity in all parts of the world. Rigorously trained in Scholasticism, the sciences and humanities, the Jesuits have also been leaders in Roman Catholic education. Their power in Europe in the 17th and 18th Centuries brought upon them the enmity of many rulers and anti-Catholic elements, and in the late 18th Century the order was virtually driven out of the Catholic world. Reinstatement came in 1814. Since then the Jesuits have flourished and now run a large number of Catholic schools and universities. They form the world's largest religious order.

to his wants." Each mission was headed by a priest, known to the Indians as the *paí-tuyá* (old father), aided by a curate, or *paí-miní* (young father). In each *reducción* the Indians had, on the Spanish model, a *cabildo*, or council. This body was composed of a *corregidor* (magistrate or mayor) and a number of other officials who were in theory elected by the whole community, but who in fact were usually appointed by the priests. The priests in most *reducciones* rigidly organized the Indians' lives, but their rule was generally benevolent and *reducción* Indians lived more secure and happy lives than they otherwise would have.

The parallel with communism comes from their economic system, which was collectivist. At first all land was held and worked in common. Later the land was divided between the *aba-mbaé* (Indian property), or private plots, and *tupá-mbaé* (God's property), which belonged to the community. The *tupá-mbaé* was maintained five days a week by regularly assigned workers and for the other two by the whole community. Its produce went to the Church, to widows and orphans, and to the destitute and the needy—thus, in embryo form, anticipating by hundreds of years the welfare state. This precocious civilization also attained a high level of culture; its statues, tapestries and paintings are today in the museums of Europe and America; one mission Indian, Nicolás Yapuguay, wrote two religious books in an era when most Spaniards were still illiterate; another edited a *History of Yapeyú;* a third composed a drama about original sin.

BY 1767, apart from 30 missions in the Paraná-Uruguay basin, with more than 100,000 converts, the Jesuits had 15 *reducciones* in the Gran Chaco and numerous others elsewhere in Latin America. The success of this "empire within an empire" caused jealousy among the Spanish settlers, who coveted the labor of the mission Indians and the large tracts of land owned by the Jesuits. When slave raiders from Brazil attacked the *reducciones,* the Spanish settlers made little effort to defend them. For once the Spanish Crown was in agreement with the Creoles. In Europe almost all the religious orders were having trouble with the secular authorities as the concepts of a supranational "Christendom," in

which the spiritual power was paramount, increasingly gave way to the modern concept of the nation-state, with authority vested in a secular monarch. The religious orders naturally resisted this secularizing tendency, and of these resisters the Jesuits were the most determined and the cleverest.

The Creole landowners' complaints gave Charles III of Spain the excuse he wanted to limit the activities of these troublesome priests, and in 1767 he signed a decree banishing the Jesuits from all Spanish territory and ordering the seizure of their property. The decree was quickly made effective, and the Indians reverted painfully to their old way of life or became peons on the large *estancias*. The Jesuit buildings fell into ruin and became covered by tropical vegetation, the cattle died or were dispersed among new owners, and the orchards and fields were reclaimed by the jungle. The first great experiment in civilizing the River Plate had come to nothing.

BUT while political advance, of which the Jesuit experiment formed a part, came virtually to a standstill, economic development—however much it had been discouraged at first by the Spanish Government, except where precious metals were concerned—managed slowly to forge ahead. From the earliest days of colonization, the cattle industry, which eventually formed the basis of the River Plate's wealth, had begun to grow.

The first livestock were brought to Buenos Aires in 1536 by Pedro de Mendoza. When Buenos Aires was abandoned in 1541, some of the pigs from its breeding station were taken to Asunción, followed by a shipment of mares and foals. Later, another expedition brought the first sheep and goats across the mountains from Peru. Finally, in 1555, the first cattle reached Paraguay—a bull and four or five cows brought from Bolivia by two Portuguese.

Within 10 years cattle abounded in Paraguay; one of the conditions that the Viceroy of Peru demanded before approving Juan Ortíz de Zárate in 1565 as Governor of Paraguay was that he increase these numbers "by putting into the said *Gobernación* . . . four thousand head of cattle, four thousand sheep, horses, mares and goats." Nevertheless, the principal product of Paraguay throughout the colonial era was yerba maté, or Paraguayan tea, and it was in the seaboard regions to the southeast that the cattle industry, and the attendant proliferation of horses, was destined to grow up.

It was the enlightened Governor Hernandarias who had the foresight to realize the potential value of stock raising, even though at the time and for many years afterward the only export market was for hides and horns, the meat (until effective salting methods were developed) being good only for local consumption. In 1603 Hernandarias shipped downstream to what is now Uruguay 100 head of cattle and 100 horses and mares, which were allowed to run wild and multiply. The initiative paid off, and the herds increased prolifically in the almost empty interior. Gauchos crossed the river from Buenos Aires to kill the cattle and sell the hides. On their heels came merchants who organized the trade and set up trading posts and then *estancias*.

But Uruguay was still largely wild, unexplored country, and it was around Buenos Aires that agriculture and stock raising first became established. Almost as soon as Juan de Garay had refounded the city in 1580, he set aside land on its periphery for cultivation and pasturage.

IN spite of the self-protective restrictions put on South American trade by the Spanish Crown, the economic interests of the colonists were bound to win in the long run. Cattle in the River Plate were officially the property of the state, but in practice they belonged to the first person who could round them up. The state issued cattle permits only to those settlers engaged in the hide industry. Soon, however, this industry, which began on a small and primitive scale, had become a major source of wealth; by the end of the 18th Century the Viceroyalty was exporting 800,000 hides a year, not all of them destined, as legally they should have been, for Spain.

Between 1748 and 1753 Buenos Aires exported local products valued at 1,620,752 pesos fuertes, or hard pesos. Between 1792 and 1796, however, 268 ships left the port of Buenos Aires with 3,790,585 cowhides and 7,800 horses, with a total value of 7,879,968 pesos fuertes. In short, trade had increased fivefold in less than half a century, without counting the contraband sent to countries prohibited to the holders of Spanish permits.

The exigencies of economic facts forced the Spanish Government to relax its stranglehold on the trade of the River Plate and to wink at the violation of the many restrictive regulations which still remained. But this gradual economic liberalization did not satisfy the demand of the colonists for more say in political administration. The Gauchos and remote country dwellers were not very concerned about this, since they paid little if any attention to the law, but they were greatly in the minority, and on the citizens of Buenos Aires and Asunción the hand of Madrid lay heavily.

BUT in this area, too, Spain was forced gradually to give way. In 1620 the Province of Buenos Aires (the city and the northern half of modern Argentina) was removed from the jurisdiction of inland Asunción, though it remained within the Viceroyalty of Peru and its governors were answerable to the Crown's representative in Lima. In 1644 the *comuneros*, or common people, of Paraguay rose in revolt against the Spanish governor and the viceroy and were not subdued for six years. Their real grievance was against the Jesuits, who owned so much land that the country's economy was being strangled. In 1717 they rose again, this time with the governor on their side. Once more the *comuneros* lost the fight, though they gained a moral victory. In a *cabildo abierto*, or open town meeting, the citizens of Asunción repudiated the nomination of Diego de los Reyes Balmaseda as the Governor and resolved *"acatar pero no cumplir"* (to respect but not to comply with) the Government's orders. It was a historic decision and, had Spain had the wit to see it, spelled the eventual doom of Spanish rule in America.

Spain's troubles were not only with its disgruntled colonists. After the relatively peaceful years that followed its conquest of South America, Spain was beginning to tangle with outsiders both at home and abroad. The first incident involved the Portuguese, now firmly settled in Brazil and not inclined to pay much attention to the boundary laid down by the Treaty of Tordesillas. In 1680 a Portuguese expedition arrived on the Uruguayan shore of the River Plate and set up an encampment called Colonia del Sacramento, on the site of the modern city of Colonia, immediately opposite Buenos Aires.

In 1701 the War of the Spanish Succession broke out between France and Spain on the one hand and England, the Netherlands, Austria, several German states and eventually Portugal on the other. The war spread to the Americas, and Spain captured the primitive settlement of Colonia. As happened so often, however, Spain won the battle but lost the war. By the Treaty of Utrecht, signed in 1713, it lost its large non-Spanish territories in Europe, and though it retained most of its colonial empire (in which its enemies showed surprisingly little interest), it had to give strategically dangerous Colonia back to Portugal. To neutralize Colonia, the Spaniards founded Montevideo in 1726. By a treaty signed in 1750 Spain regained Colonia but in return lost a great tract of what is now eastern Uruguay and southern Brazil. The area included seven Indian missions, and 30,000 Christianized Indians had to be removed to the west bank of the river, leaving to the Portuguese "all their houses, churches, buildings and property and possessions in the territory."

In 1752 the Indians rose in the so-called Guarani War, and it took the combined local forces of Spain and Portugal, united against the native menace, until 1756 to suppress them. But this did not bring peace to the River Plate. Shortly thereafter Spain found itself embroiled in the Seven Years' War. The main colonial territories in contention were those of Britain and France in North America and India, but fighting spread to the Plate and Colonia again twice changed hands, being reoccupied by the Spaniards in 1762, together with additional Uruguayan territory. But in the Treaty of Paris, Colonia was handed back to Portugal. The inhabitants of Colonia, whose morale tended to be low at the best of times, accepted the change-over passively.

All these events began to convince Spain that it could not keep its sprawling American empire intact

---

DISSOLUTION OF SPAIN'S EMPIRE

In the 16th Century, Spain had a vast empire; Spanish fleets sailed every ocean; and a fabulous supply of gold flowed in from the New World. In Europe, Spain controlled the Netherlands, Milan, Sardinia, Portugal and Naples. Then a series of disastrous wars began to dissolve the empire. Much of the Netherlands was lost in the mid-16th Century. Spain's supremacy on the sea was destroyed with the Armada in 1588. The Thirty Years' War (1618-1648) and a further conflict with France sapped Spain's strength and made France the leading Continental power. Portugal regained its independence in 1640. When King Charles II, a Hapsburg, named a member of the Bourbon dynasty as his successor, the War of the Spanish Succession broke out, and by 1714 Spain had lost Milan and Sardinia. In Latin America's wars of independence most of the New World was lost.

---

without the active support of the colonists, and this could only be obtained by making some concessions to their demands. The most notable of these concessions was the establishment of the Viceroyalty of the River Plate, separated at last from Peru and administered from Buenos Aires. But, like most such Spanish gestures, this one not only was too little but was certainly too late.

The year was 1776, and before the first viceroy had been installed, news had reached the River Plate that the 13 British colonies in North America had declared their independence in words which could not fail to find an echo when they reached Buenos Aires, Montevideo and Asunción: "We hold these truths to be self-evident, that all men are created equal, that they are endowed by their creator with certain inalienable rights, that among these are life, liberty and the pursuit of happiness. That to secure these rights governments are instituted among men, deriving their just powers from the consent of the governed. That whenever any form of government becomes destructive to those ends, it is the right of the people to alter or abolish it. . . ." To anyone for whom these words are not dulled by familiarity, America's Declaration of Independence sounds radical enough today; to an 18th Century Spanish Government it must have sounded like black heresy, and to the colonists like heady wine. Just as the North American revolutionaries considered that they were being denied their rights as *Englishmen*, the River Plate colonists objected to the denial of their rights as *Spaniards*.

But if the North American Revolution stirred feelings of unrest in the River Plate, the French Revolution in 1789 had an even more unsettling effect. Here was a full-blown revolution in one of the great monarchic and colonizing powers of Europe. In fact, even before the French Revolution itself broke out,

French revolutionary ideas had already seeped into the colonies by way of the works of Voltaire and Rousseau, which, like Tom Paine's *Rights of Man*, were smuggled into the River Plate past a strict but not always vigilant Spanish censorship.

However, it was the British who, with characteristic inadvertence, finally put the match to the fuse which the North Americans and the French had laid. On June 8, 1806, a British fleet of warships and troop transports appeared in the River Plate. For many years the British Government had noted the rising discontent of the Creoles and had toyed with the idea of coming to their aid, not from any abstract belief in colonial freedom but from a desire to open new markets for British trade—and to discomfit their hereditary European rival and enemy, Spain.

HOWEVER, this was no well-planned expedition conceived in London, but the private scheme of Commodore Sir Home Popham of the Royal Navy and Colonel William Carr Beresford of the 71st Regiment of Foot. These officers, unhampered by the kind of instant communications that restrain subordinate commanders today, had set sail early in 1806 from Cape Town with five warships and five troop transports with the idea not of liberating anybody in the modern sense, but of adding the River Plate area to the British Empire.

On June 25 an augmented force, now numbering some 1,600 men, was put ashore at the pueblo of Quilmes, today a commuting suburb of Buenos Aires, and within two days it had occupied the viceregal capital—the Spanish Viceroy, the Marquis of Sobremonte, having taken himself off to Córdoba as soon as he heard of the landings. Beresford issued a communiqué to the inhabitants guaranteeing them the right to administer their own justice and promising respect for private property, freedom for the Roman Catholic religion and freedom of commerce. He and Popham sent off jubilant reports about the "New Arcadia" to London, together with more than one million dollars in prize money.

The rejoicing, however, was a little premature. Despite Beresford's offers of a new deal, the Creoles had no wish to exchange a Spanish master for a British one. Helped by a Frenchman in Spain's service, Santiago Liniers, they proceeded to bottle up the British

in the center of the city and to force them to surrender, leaving their arms and (dreadful disgrace!) their regimental colors, which can still be seen displayed in the Church of Santo Domingo in Buenos Aires.

The success of this operation, known in Argentine history as the *Defensa,* suggested to the Creoles two things: first, they could not rely for their defense on the Spaniards; second, if they could defeat the British, perhaps they could get rid of the Spaniards, too. The following year they were to have further confirmation of these hypotheses. In February a British force, unable to reach Buenos Aires, captured and occupied Montevideo. In May another British force, under General Whitelocke, landed on the Argentine shore and on July 5 attacked Buenos Aires with about 6,000 men. Opposing them were the 50,000 *porteño* civilians and Liniers' 8,000 militiamen, largely Gauchos. The civilians and the Gauchos won, and in a single day the British Army lost 401 killed, 649 wounded and 1,924 prisoners of war. On July 7 Whitelocke signed an agreement with Liniers under which the entire British expedition, on both sides of the river, withdrew from the territory of the River Plate. This episode became known as the *Reconquista.*

APART from confirming the lessons of the *Defensa,* the second British invasion had a more positive effect. The Creoles of Montevideo noted with surprise that their British occupiers could read what they liked, say what they liked, trade with whom they liked, and—if Home Popham's conduct was any guide—virtually do what they liked, and they were perfectly prepared to give the same freedom to the occupied. Some of the Creoles had already learned of this from the clandestine visits of British merchant ships. Indeed, it was a desire to be free to trade with English merchants that helped fuel the anger against Spain and the desire to be independent. The British, with a precocious understanding of psychological warfare, were quick to drive this point home by publishing during the occupation a Spanish-language newspaper, *La Estrella del Sur (Southern Star),* which lost no opportunity to underline the contrary attitude of the Spaniards.

When the ships sailed away, the newspaper ceased publication. But the seeds of rebellion—and independence—had been sown.

Argentine landowner Ignacio Pirovano muses in the vaulted hall of his family mansion in Buenos Aires, which is now a museum.

The Legacy of Argentina's Great Empire Builders

Once people spoke wistfully of being "as rich as an Argentine." The phrase was justified. In the early 19th Century, enterprising Spanish, British, Italian and Irish immigrants carved out of the wilderness ranches, or *estancias,* so vast that the owners could gallop for days without coming to the end of their land. Their sons and grandsons built magnificent mansions, kept dozens of servants and regularly toured Europe. Though most great *estancias* have been broken up by land-dividing inheritance laws, some imposing ones remain, such as that owned by Ignacio Pirovano, shown on the following pages.

WITH HIS MOTHER, Ignacio Pirovano, scion of one of Argentina's distinguished families, discusses family business in the presence of his sister *(left)*. A cultured man about town,

Pirovano divides his time between the family's *estancia*, or ranch—where he raises beef cattle and purebred Holstein dairy cattle—and Buenos Aires, where he owns a furniture factory.

IN HIS APARTMENT, Pirovano stands by the curtained alcove that serves as his bedroom. He and his mother and sister occupy two of the building's floors and employ two butlers.

ON HIS "ESTANCIA," an 8,682-acre ranch, Pirovano wears riding clothes *(opposite)* as he prepares to inspect his cattle. The *estancia* is located 235 miles southwest of Buenos Aires.

54

GAUCHO-STYLE LIFE *of rugged simplicity is still led by peones, or workers, on Pirovano's estancia*

LASSOING A STEER from horseback, a farm hand skillfully twirls a rope. Argentine cowboys are also expert at throwing *boleadoras:* three stone or iron balls which are attached to thongs.

BRONCO-BUSTING is still done in the traditional way by lassoing the wild horse, blindfolding it *(above)* and tying it to a post. Then some brave *peón* mounts for a jolting ride.

DRIVING CATTLE by a windbreak of trees *(below)*, ranch hands ride through dust kicked up from the dry soil. Pirovano has 1,500 beef cattle and 500 dairy cattle on his *estancia*.

FOLK DANCING by *peones* entertains Pirovano and his guests *(background)*. The workers live well, getting free food and shelter, although they make only $40 a month.

A RELAXED HOUSEWIFE, Angelica Carabassa knits during the evening in a living room decorated with shields, lances and a suit of armor. She is from a family of wealthy jewelers.

AN ACTIVE MOTHER, Mrs. Carabassa *(opposite)* takes a ride in a pony cart with her children on the lawn of her estate near Buenos Aires. Her husband's family once owned 1.5 million acres.

A CAREFUL PLANNER visiting her kitchen, Mrs. Carabassa supervises the cooking. Argentine aristocrats used to keep huge domestic staffs—even a lackey who only polished the silver.

AN ELEGANT HOSTESS, Mrs. Carabassa presides over high tea —a British custom adopted by wealthy Argentines. Her husband still keeps a few cattle and is an expert on cattle breeding.

59

On a sunlit day in 1892 top-hatted dignitaries and soldiers in full dress wait in Buenos Aires' Plaza del Mayo for the president to emerge

from his executive offices in the Casa Rosada, or Government Palace.

4

Libertad, Libertad, Libertad!

ON the 25th of May, 1810, a date commemorated in the names of streets and squares throughout Argentina, the people of Buenos Aires took the first decisive step on the road to independence. Standing in a light drizzle, a crowd of Creole citizens waited outside the Cabildo, or city hall, where the city councilors were in session, and in an unprecedented and dramatic assertion of democracy demanded: *"El pueblo quiere saber de qué se trata"* (The people want to know what is being discussed).

This unheard-of insubordination was to have as unexpected, and almost as wide, repercussions as the Boston Tea Party, and like that protest, it was triggered by events in faraway Europe. In 1808 Napoleon's troops had invaded Spain, and by 1810 the news had reached Buenos Aires that the French had captured Seville, the last important city in the Peninsula to remain in Spanish hands. This placed the newly arrived Spanish Viceroy to the River Plate, Don Baltasar Hidalgo de Cisneros, in a position of very dubious authority, and on May 22, 1810, a *cabildo abierto*, or open council of leading citizens,

was convoked to discuss where authority should rest—with a Viceroy who now represented no government or with the constituted authorities of the city of Buenos Aires.

At an earlier meeting between the Viceroy and civil and military authorities, one Army commander, a Colonel Merlo, had declared that he and his men were prepared to die for the Viceroy. To this Colonel Cornelio Saavedra retorted that in Europe only Cádiz and the Isla de León were still Spanish. "And so, sir? Cádiz and the Isla de León are Spain? And does this immense territory [and] its millions of inhabitants have to recognize the sovereignty of the merchants of Cádiz and fishermen of the Isla de León. . . . No, sir, . . . we have resolved to reassume our rights and keep them for ourselves."

THE well-to-do civilians of the *cabildo abierto,* however, proved to be a good deal more cautious than the outspoken Colonel Saavedra, and for three days they argued nervously as the crowds outside in the plaza grew larger and more restive, shouting *"Que se vote! Que se vote!"* (Vote! Vote!) and *"Abajo Cisneros!"* (Down with Cisneros!).

On the fourth day, May 25, in the face of the insistent demand to know *de qué se trata,* the *cabildo abierto* announced that it was nominating a new junta, or acting administration, with Colonel Saavedra as president. Thus the first American-appointed Government in the River Plate was established. The Viceroy, already deprived of his titles and even of his former naval rank, was unceremoniously shipped off to the Canary Islands.

But in spite of this dramatic gesture, with its overtones of the French Revolution, the people of the River Plate and their self-appointed representatives were still of two minds about what or whom they were fighting for, or even against. The monarchic tradition remained strong. In fact, this theoretical loyalty to the Crown was to plague and divide the Spanish American nations throughout their long war of independence, causing wars within a war and a plethora of congresses and constitutions. Fortunately, however, while the inexperienced and theoretical-minded politicians argued, the soldiers of the revolution, under the brilliant leadership of the famous liberator José de San Martín, got on with the job of clearing out the Spaniards. San Martín, unlike many subsequent South American military men, never allowed his political views to interfere with his military duties. He was the first of a small number of larger-than-life characters who, despite the *cabildos* and congresses and talk of democracy, were to shape the destiny of the new nations.

José de San Martín was born in February 1778 in Yapeyú, in northern Argentina, but his early career was spent in the service of Spain. At the age of 11 his "precocious vocation" for the career of arms led to his acceptance by Madrid as a cadet in the Murcia Regiment, in which he saw service in North Africa, fighting against the Moors. His next battles were against the French, and in 1795 he won a battlefield commission as a lieutenant. He rose steadily in rank, and in June 1811 he was given command of a regiment. But in September of that year—having heard of the events of 1810 in Buenos Aires—San Martín decided to give up his commission and to sail for home, where he arrived in March 1812 after an absense of 27 years. On his arrival in Buenos Aires he found something much like political anarchy, with arguments raging between proponents of a strong central government and those who wanted a loose federal system—another question that was to plague the River Plate, like the United States, for many years to come. For San Martín all this was, for the time being, irrelevant; what mattered first was military victory over the armies of Spain. So, bypassing the squabbling *políticos*, he founded, together with General Carlos de Alvear, a secret patriotic society, the Logia Lautaro.

This powerful quasi-military pressure group was to set a dangerous precedent in Latin America, and the repercussions are felt to this day, but at the time it gave San Martín a most necessary means of forcing the politicians to do what was militarily expedient. He was shortly entrusted with the organization of a squadron of cavalry that became the famous Regimiento de Granaderos a Caballo and the nucleus of the patriot armies. Then, setting up his headquarters at El Retiro, near Buenos Aires, San Martín founded a school of military tactics and discipline and began forging the army that would win independence.

ALTHOUGH a rising similar to that in Buenos Aires had occurred in the same year in Caracas, Venezuela, and there had been parallel stirrings in Mexico, Spanish forces were still in firm control of the rest of the continent. Their headquarters were in Lima, and it soon became evident to San Martín that the River Plate could not be free and safe from reconquest unless the war was carried across the Andes into Peru itself—a conviction also reached by Simón Bolívar, the great Venezuelan revolutionary leader.

Until the arrival of San Martín, the patriots' military actions had been sporadic and as uncoordinated as the activities of the politicians. San Martín changed all this. In 1813 the Government in Buenos Aires, under pressure from San Martín's Logia Lautaro, called a general constituent assembly that officially took over the former sovereign powers of the Spanish Crown in the name of the United Provinces of the River Plate. An astonishing list of reforms was enacted, including the abolition of torture and of titles of nobility. New legislation provided for representative government, freedom of the individual and freedom of the press.

On the military side, San Martín also acted swiftly. Early in 1813 news reached Buenos Aires that a Spanish expedition had slipped upriver past the city bound for San Lorenzo. San Martín immediately left Buenos Aires at the head of 120 chosen grenadiers and found the Spanish ships lying offshore 14 miles north of Rosario. On the morning of February 3 the Spaniards began to disembark. For the first time the bugle of the grenadiers sounded the attack. After a hand-to-hand battle, the grenadiers routed the Spaniards, who retired to their ships leaving behind their colors and some valuable arms. As an Argentine historian puts it with pardonable patriotic hindsight: "This [battle] marks the point of departure of [San Martín's] great continental campaign, whose theater of operations was South America, across rivers, pampas, mountains and seas."

The next year, in 1814, San Martín transferred his activities to the city of Mendoza, where for two and a half years he prepared his Army of the Andes. He enlisted troops locally and raised local taxes to pay for them. To equip his forces he built an arsenal, a powder factory and a textile mill. By January of 1817 he was ready, and he set out toward the forbidding barrier of the Cordillera with 4,000 regular troops and an auxiliary militia of 1,400. Ahead of them lay a range with peaks more than 20,000 feet high covered by perpetual snow and negotiable by only five

TWO POST-INDEPENDENCE DICTATORS

Juan Manuel de Rosas ruled Argentina from 1829 to 1831 and from 1835 to 1852. He governed by terror, ruthlessly executing his rivals, and bribed with huge grants of land the *estancieros* who supported him. Opponents finally fought and routed his conscripted army, and Rosas fled to England, where he died in 1877. Francisco Solano López was dictator of Paraguay from 1862 to 1870, when he was shot at the end of a disastrous, hopeless war which had decimated the country's male population. López was vain, dissipated and belligerent. Like Rosas, he was able to stay in power only by repression.

ROSAS

LOPEZ

passes on a 500-mile front. Heavy cannons had to be dragged over the passes at altitudes up to 12,000 feet. It was such an impossible enterprise that the Spaniards in Chile were taken unprepared. On February 12 San Martín's forces surprised the Spaniards at Chacabuco and defeated them. Two days later San Martín entered the Chilean capital, Santiago. He was welcomed as a savior by the Chilean people and was offered supreme political office, which he refused. On April 5, 1818, he won a second and decisive victory over the Spanish at Maipú. Chile was now free, and the road was open to Peru, the seat of Spain's remaining power.

AFTER the triumph at Maipú, San Martín went back to Buenos Aires to obtain money, supplies and men to continue his campaign. There he found the political situation as chaotic as before. Paraguay in 1813 had declared its independence from the United Provinces; Uruguay was in the grip of civil war and was having trouble not only with the Spaniards but also with the Portuguese. And in Argentina, there was increasing strife between the independent-minded provinces and the central Government in Buenos Aires.

Nevertheless, San Martín returned to Chile, and with the blessing of Bernardo O'Higgins, the Chilean chief of state, and the cooperation of Admiral Lord Cochrane, the Scottish-born commander of the Chilean Navy, he set sail for Peru in August 1820 with eight warships and 16 transports carrying 4,700 troops. The revolutionary flotilla blockaded Callao, Lima's port, and that, together with poor morale and a "fifth column" in Lima itself, led to capitulation and the entry of San Martín into the viceregal capital on July 10, 1821.

A year after this decisive victory, in July 1822, San Martín and his great counterpart Simón Bolívar, who had liberated Colombia and Ecuador, met in the Ecuadoran city of Guayaquil. The meeting was unfruitful, however, and San Martín, fearful that lack of cooperation between himself and Bolívar would jeopardize their joint war against Spain, decided to bow out and return to Argentina.

His re-entry into Buenos Aires was a sad one. His wife had died while he was on his way home. The various factions in the River Plate all clamored for his help, leadership or mediation, but he was disillusioned with politics and politicians. On February 10, 1824, he sailed for Europe, promising to return whenever "the Sovereigns of Europe try to interfere in our affairs." He was still more disillusioned when he did return in 1829. During the time he had been in Europe, Argentina had fought a war with Brazil, and the people were bitter that he had not come home to help. When his ship entered the harbor of Buenos Aires, it was met with a reception so cold that San Martín did not even disembark, but transferred to another ship and sailed back to Europe. He died in 1850 in self-imposed exile in France.

San Martín had good reason for his disillusionment with Argentina's politicians. While he had waged war, inept government had succeeded inept government in Buenos Aires and the Argentine provinces had rebelled and declared themselves autonomous political units. An assembly called to thrash out a new constitution had labored long and then, under pressure from powerful Buenos Aires, had written one calling for a strong centralized government. It was quickly rejected by a majority of the provinces, and this led to sporadic civil war which was to continue until the middle of the century.

TWO of the most important provinces, Uruguay and Paraguay, had been in any case as good as lost. Their otherwise disparate histories are linked by another of the great figures of South American independence, José Gervasio Artigas. Born in 1764 in Montevideo, Artigas came from a family that had taken part in the first settlement in 1726 and had become what amounted to landed gentry. Such families, though they had town houses in Montevideo, lived the life of the frontier, mostly on horseback in the plains around their *estancias,* the children spending more time in the company of Gauchos than in the schoolroom—although Artigas himself attended a Franciscan school in Montevideo. When he left school, he became a purveyor of hides and cattle products, selling to family friends in the export trade. He was also a notable smuggler—then, as now, a rather admired occupation in the River Plate.

But soon the young Artigas joined a regiment of mounted militia that was being raised to combat Indian raids and to repel threatened attacks by the

Portuguese from Brazil. A year later he was promoted to captain of this militia and in 1799 became adjutant of a regiment in Montevideo.

A crisis in Artigas' life came in 1810. Like many of his fellow Orientales, he was disgruntled by the high-handed ways of the viceregal Government in Buenos Aires, and especially by its discrimination against Montevideo in commercial matters. Therefore when the news of the overthrow of Viceroy Cisneros by the Buenos Aires *cabildo abierto* of 1810 reached Montevideo, Artigas was stirred by enthusiasm for this move toward independence. His enthusiasm turned to black disappointment when not only the Spanish governor of Montevideo but also the local *cabildo* repudiated the Buenos Aires action and decided instead to recognize the rump Government in what was left of Spain. When in the following year a new viceroy of the River Plate was warmly welcomed in Montevideo, and when this viceroy declared war on Buenos Aires, Artigas had had enough.

Leaving his military post, he went to Buenos Aires, where he offered his services to the junta to "carry the standard of liberty to the walls of Montevideo." Soon sporadic rebellions began breaking out all over the Banda Oriental (Uruguay), and apart from Montevideo, only the city of Colonia remained loyal to the viceroy. In April 1811 Artigas crossed the river into Uruguay at Paysandú, oppposite Entre Ríos, and issued a stirring proclamation to his countrymen: ". . . and may those tyrants tremble who have incurred our wrath, without realizing that the Americans of the South are ready to defend their country, and rather to die with honor than to live in ignominy and humiliating captivity." He had of course no mandate or commission from anybody in the Banda Oriental, but his hawk nose and his independent Gaucho manner were familiar throughout the country and within weeks he became the generally accepted leader of the revolutionaries.

BUT a further disappointment awaited Artigas and his followers. Making an almost complete about-face, the Government in Buenos Aires concluded an armistice with Montevideo, agreed to recognize the sovereignty of the king of Spain, and promised to withdraw its troops from the Banda Oriental and half of Entre Ríos. The politicians in

Buenos Aires had several practical reasons for making these concessions at this time, but to Artigas and the Orientales it was simple treachery, and the shock of it turned the Banda Oriental into a nation.

Artigas withdrew his troops as ordered, but in his own way and with his own purposes. His intention was to preserve his army intact—so that it might return to reconquer the country and found an independent Uruguay. The soldiers did not travel alone. Rather than submit again to the Spaniards, four fifths of the population of the Banda Oriental joined the trek into exile in Entre Ríos. In an astonishing mass movement, which was later called the Exodus of the Orientales, entire families left their homes and possessions, piled their few movable goods into ox wagons and joined Artigas' retreating army.

But Artigas and the Orientales had not been in Entre Ríos very long when the armistice between Buenos Aires and the viceroy was shattered and troops from Argentina crossed the river to besiege Montevideo. Artigas joined in the siege and, after the capitulation of the viceroy's army, managed also to get rid of the troops from Buenos Aires.

UNFORTUNATELY, just as Uruguayan independence seemed to be assured, Artigas got the notion of annexing certain segments of Brazilian territory. The Brazilians attacked, and after four years of fighting, Artigas was forced to flee into exile in Paraguay. The next year, in 1821, Brazil annexed Uruguay, and it was not until 1828 that a heroic patriot army, aided by Buenos Aires, succeeded in once more liberating the country. In 1829 a constituent assembly produced a constitution, and on July 18, 1830, this document, establishing the Estado Oriental del Uruguay, was officially adopted. Today Montevideo's principal boulevard, Avenida 18 de Julio, commemorates Uruguay's independence from both Brazil and the United Provinces.

Meanwhile Paraguay had drifted even farther from the Buenos Aires fold. The Paraguayans had still more reason than the Orientales for feeling separate from (and rather superior to) the other provinces. Their part-Guarani culture and universally spoken Guarani language set them apart, and the fact that Asunción had for so many years been the dominant River Plate city made them unwilling to accept the leadership of parvenu Buenos Aires. Thus Paraguay was highly enthusiastic when, in 1814, Artigas broke with Buenos Aires and proposed a common front against the central Government.

In the previous year the provincial government in Asunción had been replaced by the rule of two consuls (the first consul being given the title of Caesar, and the second that of Pompey), and the name of the province had been changed to the Republic of Paraguay. Buenos Aires begged the Paraguayans to stay within the River Plate family, but Paraguay, encouraged by Artigas, had made up its mind to remain independent. This was perhaps fortunate for the rest of the River Plate, since the First Consul, José de Francia, hardened into an uncompromising dictator, and except for intervals of anarchy, dictatorship was all Paraguay was to know for more than a century.

THUS independence came to the River Plate, but in a form the reverse of *e pluribus unum*. Even within the three separate countries dissension ruled. Argentina presented a picture of total disarray. The Constitution of 1819 had reduced the provinces to administrative units, ignoring the fact that they represented armed centers of local power and could disregard Buenos Aires with impunity. A number of them were shortly in virtual revolt. The following year, 1820, went down in history as "The Terrible Year" or "The Year of Anarchy." There was no effective national government, and the most important province, Buenos Aires, had 24 provincial governments between February and November—an average of more than two a month.

At this point Colonel Manuel Dorrego stepped in to restore order. A city-bred Army officer, Dorrego had angered his fellow townsmen by his too sympathetic attitude toward the Gauchos, whom they regarded as little better than savages, and he had been exiled to the United States. Now he returned to clear up the mess that his compatriots had made.

He ordered elections in the key Province of Buenos Aires, which brought Martín Rodríguez, a hero of the *Defensa* and the *Reconquista* (see Chapter 3), and Bernardino de Rivadavia, a former member of the government, back onto the national scene. Rivadavia has been called "the Alexander Hamilton

of the Argentine Revolution." His aim was a state with the democratic structure of the United States, but with a strong central government able to control and promote the country's financial and mercantile activity. Rivadavia was rightly acclaimed for his part in bringing some semblance of order to Argentina, but Dorrego's part in bringing this about was not much appreciated by his contemporaries, who never forgave him for his overdemocratic proclivities. In 1828 he was toppled from his post as Governor of Buenos Aires by a group including Rivadavia himself and was subsequently shot. As a result of the shooting of Dorrego, the provinces once more rose against the capital, and civil war was ended the next year, 1829, only by the installation of Juan Manuel de Rosas as dictator.

Rosas, who was to rule for 20 years, is one of the most contradictory figures in Argentine history. A federalist, or supporter of provincial rights, he became an absolute and tyrannical ruler. Owing his support to the Gauchos and the urban working classes, he himself was a rich man, an *estanciero*, and owned a meat-salting plant and a fleet of ships to carry its products abroad. During his years of power, Rosas became a terrifying figure. He imprisoned or executed thousands of people and drove thousands of others into exile in Uruguay and Chile. He divided the land of his political enemies among his supporters. The Gauchos, who had supported him, were forbidden to hunt wild cattle or horses and were reduced to the status of agricultural laborers.

BUT, whatever his crimes and faults, Rosas did succeed in doing one thing: he transformed Argentina into a nation and aroused Argentine patriotism by his spirited resistance to highhanded attempts by both Britain and France to influence politics in the River Plate. But success made Rosas overconfident. In 1851, deciding that it was time to bring Paraguay and Uruguay back into the fold, he sent out a formal letter to provincial governors tendering his resignation, a familiar prelude to taking further dictatorial powers. This time someone took him seriously. The Governor of Entre Ríos, General Justo José de Urquiza, accepted the resignation. This defiance rallied the dictator's opponents, and on February 3, 1852, his conscripted forces were decisively beaten by those of

Governor Urquiza at the battle of Monte Caseros.

The defeat of Rosas led to still another period of conflict. In an attempt to settle some of the nation's problems, a congress convened in 1853 to draft a new constitution. The resulting document, which, with minor modifications, remains in force to this day, was acceptable to the provinces but not to Buenos Aires, and a civil war broke out. In 1859 Buenos Aires was defeated and agreed to join the confederation. However, just as it appeared that Argentina was settling down to some political peace, war broke out with Paraguay.

IN the years since its 1813 declaration of independence, Paraguay had been ruled largely by dictators, benevolent and otherwise, the most recent of them having been Carlos Antonio López, an enlightened despot who managed to stay in office from 1841 to 1862, and only relinquished the presidency on his death. During his rule, he persuaded a British firm to build one of the first railroads in South America, invited foreign technicians and professional men to settle in Paraguay and, not so happily, sent his son, Francisco Solano López, a precocious general (at 18), to buy armaments in Europe.

Still more unhappily, when López died in 1862, he was succeeded by his son. López the second was a megalomaniacal dictator who came close to destroying his country. On a trip to Europe in 1853 to 1855 he had absorbed some rather hasty ideas about politics, diplomacy and military strategy. His travels, far from making him any more modest about his own or his country's importance in the world, seem to have had the opposite effect, and this arrogance precipitated the war that nearly destroyed his nation.

It all began in November 1864 when the Brazilian vessel *Marquez de Olinda* appeared in the Paraguay River carrying the new governor of Brazil's Matto Grosso State upstream to his post. López had earlier received word that Brazil had invaded Uruguay, and jumping to Uruguay's defense, he immediately interned the *Marquez de Olinda* as a belligerent vessel. He also severed diplomatic relations with Brazil.

Had López been content to leave matters there, he might have got his country involved in no worse than a minor jungle war with Brazil. But this did not fit in with his notions of glory. In an attempt to outflank the Brazilians, he marched into the Argentine Province of Corrientes, which happened to be in the way. The Argentines not unnaturally objected and in 1865 signed a secret treaty of mutual protection, grandly called the Triple Alliance, with Brazil and a now compliant Uruguay. Uruguay was an ineffective participant, but Paraguay should never have tackled its huge neighbors, Brazil and Argentina.

The fighting spirit of the Guarani had not changed, however, and for six years the beleaguered country held out. The natural belligerence and bravery of the Paraguayans were reinforced by the Draconian actions of López. Officers who retreated or allowed themselves to be beaten were executed, and their wives were forced to disown them in the press. Thousands of real or imaginary opponents and "traitors" were imprisoned, tortured and killed.

The inevitable outcome of the war was defeat for Paraguay, and on March 1, 1870, the army of the alliance encircled López and the pathetic remnants of his forces. The Brazilian General Correa da 'Cámara called out, "Surrender yourself, Marshal. Your life is guaranteed." López replied, "I die for my country, with sword in hand." And, thanks to a shot fired by a Brazilian soldier, he did. Some accounts have it that he said, "I die with my country." If so, he was nearly right. At the outset of the war, Paraguay's population had been 525,000. In 1871 it was down to 221,000, of whom only 29,000 were adult males. Paraguay has never really recovered from these crushing losses. Brazil and Argentina occupied the country for six years but could exact no reparations since Paraguay was unable to pay them.

SIGNIFICANTLY, Uruguay did not take part in the occupation. It had troubles enough of its own at home. Its condition was rather like that of England during the Wars of the Roses. Appropriately enough, the two sides in Uruguay's endemic civil war were, like the roses, Colorados (Reds) and Blancos (Whites). Today these are respectable political parties, but in the 19th Century they were warring bands with about as much ideological motivation as the rival royal houses of York and Lancaster.

The worst period of this internecine strife was the 1840s, when the periodic fighting between the Blancos and the Colorados blossomed into a full-scale war. The Blancos were led by Manuel Oribe, a one-time President of Uruguay who had fled to Argentina after being deposed by the Colorados. Taking command of the Blanco forces, Oribe invaded Uruguay in 1843 and precipitated what Uruguayans call *La Guerra Grande* (the Great War).

Its principal result was the siege of Montevideo, which lasted from 1843 to 1851 and caused the city to be called the Troy of South America. However, Montevideo did not suffer unduly, thanks to its maritime links with the outside world. Trade boomed, the theaters stayed open and social life flourished. It was "the camp" that suffered, since the cattle industry was harassed by banditry and military operations and was deprived of its principal export outlet. Thus, as in Argentina, antagonism grew between the capital and the countryside.

THE siege was lifted and peace was restored in 1851. Unfortunately, in 1863, civil war flared up again, with Brazil and Argentina intervening on behalf of the Colorados. In 1865 the outbreak of the bloody war between Paraguay and the Triple Alliance coincided with the start of 25 years of Uruguayan rule by military officers and *caudillos*, or self-appointed strongmen. This period of *militarismo* brought no stability: one of the military rulers, Colonel Lorenzo Latorre, resigned on the understandable grounds that Uruguayans were ungovernable.

He was, however, unduly pessimistic. Although the 1890s saw some turmoil, the inauguration of José Batlle y Ordóñez as President in 1903 ushered in a period of constitutional civilian rule that has lasted to this day. With Batlle, one of the greatest statesmen South America has produced (see Chapter 7), Uruguay sailed serenely into the 20th Century.

Starting with the era of the Paraguayan War, Argentina seemed to be set on the same hopeful course, though with some contrary winds. President Bartolomé Mitre, elected in 1862 under the 1853 Constitution, brought in an era of peaceful civilian rule that had an immediate effect on national development. Immigrants poured in from poverty-stricken Europe and hungry Ireland, British investors took heart again, and in Mitre's first year of office the Province of Buenos Aires granted a concession to a British company for building a 72-mile stretch of railroad, the first important link in the vast network that now covers the country.

This was the era as well of the great educator Domingo Faustino Sarmiento, who began the work that was to make Argentina rank with Uruguay educationally—they are the most literate nations in South America. As chief of the Department of Schools between 1856 and 1861, Sarmiento founded many new schools and improved the curriculum. As President from 1868 to 1874, he doubled the number of state primary schools and brought in North American teachers to organize teachers' training colleges. He founded the Exact Sciences Academy and the Schools of Mining and Agronomy. During his presidency, the country continued to prosper, more railways and telegraph lines were built, and by the end of his term, immigration figures had reached 40,000 a year.

In 1891 the first widely based "popular" political party, the Unión Cívica Radical, was founded by Leandro N. Alem and Hipólito Irigoyen. In 1912 President Roque Saenz Peña introduced universal and compulsory male suffrage, the secret ballot and a strict system of registration of voters. Under these laws, at the 1916 elections, Hipólito Irigoyen became the first Radical President of Argentina.

THE ship of state seemed to have found the fair winds presaged by the name of its capital. But there were storm clouds on the horizon. A prescient British journalist named Gordon Ross, who had worked in Buenos Aires, hinted at the nature of these clouds when he wrote in 1916: "What may happen in the present newly commenced era of compulsory exercise of a universal franchise no one can well say, but most of the landed influence still belongs to the great historic Argentine families. . . . It will be a long time . . . before the prestige of these families ceases to make its influence felt. . . ."

Ross was correct. The great landed families clung tenaciously to their wealth and power, effectively stifling all Government attempts to extend to the Argentine poor a measure of social justice and a fair share of the nation's wealth. Discontent increased until finally there was an explosion that produced the "proletarian" dictatorship of Juan Perón and the severe political unrest that has continued to this day.

Buyers on horseback appraise cattle driven in from the Pampa to Buenos Aires pens. Here as many as 25,000 are auctioned off daily.

Moving the Economy into the Twentieth Century

Through the 19th and into the 20th Century the economy of the River Plate was synonymous with the Pampa—the cattle and farm products of a few powerful families. But as the voice of the people began to be heard in politics, the economy began to broaden as well. Today intensive efforts are being made to take advantage of *all* resources. Steel mills are springing up. Some 80,000 cars a year are rolling off Argentine assembly lines. Argentina's oil deposits are being vigorously exploited. Industrializing has not been easy. In Buenos Aires, many who came to fill new jobs were met with severe housing shortages. Middle-class families, such as the Dillons *(pages 72 and 73)*, have had to work hard to offset high living costs. But the very existence of this large and literate middle class is the sign of a modern economy.

HEAVY INDUSTRY surges ahead in Argentina, pulling the economy with it

BLEAK OFFSHORE WELLS tap an oil field *(above)* near the Patagonian town of Comodoro Rivadavia, on the Atlantic coast of Argentina. As recently as 1958 the importation of oil accounted for most of the nation's unfavorable trade balance. But increased drilling, mostly by foreign oilmen, more than doubled output by 1962.

RAW BOOMTOWN of Comodoro Rivadavia *(left)* sprawls haphazardly over the Patagonian hills. Now Argentina's chief oil-producing center, with a population of more than 40,000, it owes its existence to an accident. Ranchers drilling for water in 1957 found oil instead. The town is building factories to process oil by-products.

MODERN ASSEMBLY LINE in the giant Córdoba plant *(left)* of Industrias Kaiser Argentina—a branch of the U.S. Kaiser Company—moves car bodies toward the final stages of production. IKA uses auto-part dies formerly employed in U.S. plants.

YOUTHFUL WORKERS leave the IKA Córdoba plant *(below)* on their motor-cycles. The 7,200 workers employed by this factory receive such benefits as training courses, a broad medical plan and company-sponsored sports and cultural activities.

EATING DINNER, Mr. and Mrs. Dillon and their seven children *(above)* crowd the parlor of their three-and-a-half room apartment. A housing shortage makes even cramped flats rare.

TEACHING during the morning, Hector Dillon, the head of the family *(above)*, instructs a class of young boys in geography at the small grade school of which he is the principal.

DISCUSSING PAPERS with a colleague *(below)*, Mr. Dillon labors at his afternoon job—a clerkship in the Ministry of Public Works. He needs two jobs to meet the rising cost of living.

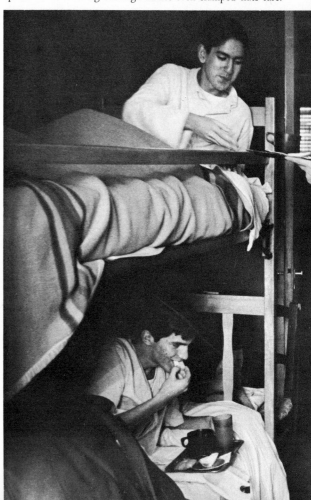

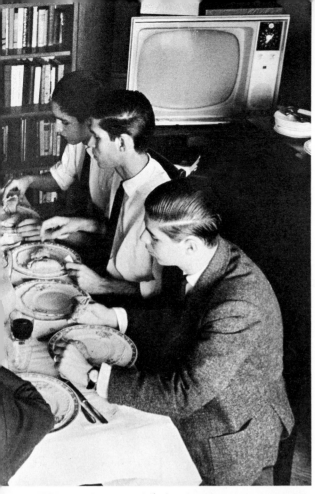

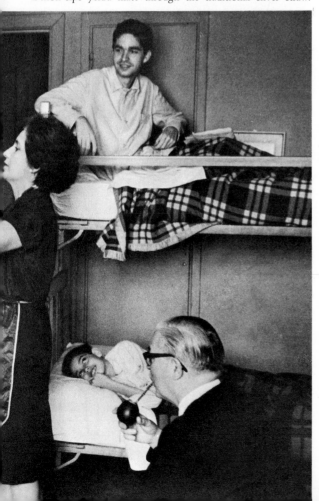

SERVING BREAKFAST in bed on Saturday morning, Mrs. Dillon *(below)* earns her sons' gratitude. At the lower right, Mr. Dillon sips yerba maté through the traditional silver straw.

MIDDLE-CLASS FAMILY, the
Dillons of Buenos Aires work hard for their livelihood

SHOPPING, Mrs. Dillon and her daughter *(above)* buy pasta for a spaghetti dinner. Argentines must endure two meatless days a week because of a law conserving beef for export.

HANGING LAUNDRY, Mrs. Dillon puts the apartment house roof to good use *(below)*. Irish family names are common in Argentina, with its thousands of immigrants from the British Isles.

URBAN POVERTY is a continuing blight in underdeveloped Paraguay and still scars such thriving cities as Buenos Aires

RUN-DOWN WATERFRONT in Asunción, Paraguay, serves as a port for the small freighters and cargo barges that ply the Paraná River, Paraguay's principal trade route to distant Buenos Aires.

GRIM SHANTYTOWNS called *villas miseria (right)* plague Buenos Aires. Accelerating industrialization after World War II brought an influx of workers who could find no other place to live.

A crowded street market teems with shoppers on a hot summer morning in Paraguay's slow-moving capital, Asunción. The market is run

ntirely by women who bring goods in from nearby farms on burros.

5

Remote and Troubled Paraguay

TO those who do not know the country, a reference to Paraguay evokes much the same response as a reference to Timbuktu; it conjures up a vision of all that is remote, foreign, backward and unknown. While the name of Argentina may call forth different stock responses from different people (tangos, pampas, Gauchos, railroad shares), it is almost sure to evoke *some* response. A mention of Paraguay will probably produce a blank stare or, possibly, a cautious "How interesting."

For this, of course, geography is partly to blame. In early colonial times, geography favored Paraguay, since Asunción was an important staging post on the route from the Viceroyalty of Peru to the River Plate. But when the coastal Plate countries established regular and direct sea communications with the outside world, landlocked Paraguay became isolated, and even with the coming of air travel it was still off the routes of the major airlines.

In addition to being isolated, Paraguay lacks other natural advantages enjoyed by Uruguay and Argentina—the vast stretches of fertile pastureland which enabled them to build up their great herds of cattle and sheep and the arable land on which wheat and other cereal crops can flourish. Other South American countries that share Paraguay's shortage of suitable stockbreeding and agricultural land have been able to compensate for it through the discovery of mineral resources and the development of industry. Paraguay is reputed to possess large deposits of petroleum and iron ore, but they have not yet been developed. As a result, industry in Paraguay is practically nonexistent, and all modern capital equipment and most consumer goods must be imported.

PARTLY as a result of its awkward, unprofitable geography, Paraguay has been plagued by a history of political instability. Between the fall of Francisco Solano López in 1870 and the election of Dr. José P. Guggiari in 1928, the country changed presidents 30 times, had two assassinations of presidents, six successful coups d'état, one unsuccessful coup d'état, three successful revolutions, eight abortive revolutions and one period (1909-1912) despairingly classified by the author of a Paraguayan textbook as "anarchy." Guggiari himself was the first President with an official opposition. A Paraguayan history book observed without comment: "It was the only presidential election in the country at which there were two candidates."

This seemed a hopeful sign for the future, but almost before the Paraguayan people could get used to the idea of having a workable two-party system, the country was forced into political unity again by the tragedy of the Chaco War. This war, against Bolivia, raged from 1932 to 1935. It was only slightly less bloody than the war against the Triple Alliance 62 years earlier, though this time Paraguay neither started it nor lost it.

Theoretically, the Chaco War was fought because of differences between Bolivia and Paraguay about the location of the boundary between them. But the precise setting of Paraguayan and Bolivian outposts in a huge region that is a desert in the dry season and a swamp in the wet was a minor consideration, and the diplomatic arguments masked the true cause of the war: Bolivia's desire to control the whole Chaco. To Paraguay this sparsely inhabited and inhospitable region was vital as a source of quebracho wood, an essential export, and for cattle grazing. To land-locked Bolivia, most of whose people live on the Altiplano, a bleak Andean plateau 13,000 feet above sea level, owning the Chaco would have provided access to a navigable river with an outlet to the Atlantic for Bolivia's major export, tin.

Militarily, because of the nature of the terrain, the Chaco War was inevitably an infantry war; the cavalry had to fight on foot and tanks were virtually useless. In the circumstances, it might have been expected that the fighting would degenerate into the static trench warfare of the Western Front in World War I. In fact, however, the Paraguayans had learned the lessons of that conflict, and the Chaco War was one of movement, foreshadowing the strategy of World War II. Indeed, the military historian David H. Zook Jr. goes so far as to say: "The return of genuine maneuver to warfare marked [the Paraguayan] Lieutenant Colonel José Félix Estigarribia as a precursor of Field Marshal Erwin Rommel."

THE war was a disaster for Bolivia. After a year and a half of fighting, the Bolivian Army in the field had been reduced from 77,000 men to 7,000. Some 6,000 Bolivians had deserted and fled to Argentina, while 10,000 were prisoners in Paraguay; 14,000 were dead and 32,000 had been evacuated because of wounds or tropical disease. In addition, although Bolivia eventually mobilized a total of 250,000 men (against Paraguay's 140,000), they were mostly untrained conscripts with no stomach for the job. The Paraguayans, on the other hand, had miraculously retained the belligerent resilience that they had shown in the 1865-1870 war against the Triple Alliance. And they possessed in Estigarribia a bold, shrewd and resourceful leader.

Many of the war's battles were short, sharp and savage. Finally in 1935, after staggering losses on both sides, Bolivia had had enough, and after mediation by Argentina, Brazil, Chile, Peru, Uruguay and the United States, an armistice was arranged. The shooting war was over, but it was not until July 21, 1938, that a peace treaty was signed, leaving Paraguay in occupation of the Chaco but guaranteeing Bolivia free transit through the territory and the right to establish customs facilities and warehouses in the Paraguayan river port of Puerto Casado.

The Bolivians, ironically, gained more than the Paraguayans in one respect; the disaster drove home to the Bolivian ruling class a realization that reforms were desperately needed, and this led to the great Bolivian social revolution of 1952. In Paraguay the male population of the country once again had been decimated. The high proportion of women to men, which in 1932 was only just beginning to be redressed after the earlier war, became as noticeable as it was in Europe after the slaughter of World War I. Paraguayan girls of polite and decorous families are still likely to inquire of male foreign visitors, "Are you married?" and on receiving an affirmative answer, to say, "What a pity." Even priests have been known to remark privately that there is a case for legalized polygamy in Paraguay.

Politically the country would appear superficially to have reverted to the days of the López family dynasty, which ruled from 1844 to 1870. After the armistice in 1935, a field commander, Colonel Rafael Franco, became President. He was followed by a succession of dictators, some of them reasonably able and some not. Then, in 1954, General Alfredo Stroessner, the son of a German immigrant, took office as President, and he has remained in office ever since. There have been two subsequent elections, but in these the opposition parties have either abstained (alleging restrictions on campaigning, incorrect electoral rolls and similar irregularities) or have cried fraud when the results were announced. The Stroessner regime has been cold-shouldered internationally as dictatorial. Although strongly anti-Communist, it has been regarded with almost as much disapproval in Washington as in Havana. It has received a limited share of aid from international or United States agencies, although the Alliance for Progress has helped build schools and roads and has provided technical assistance in rural areas.

MANY Paraguayans, including General Stroessner, feel that this discrimination is unfair. In 1962, talking to a visiting British journalist, Stroessner recounted the country's record of civil war, revolution and assassination and said: "They call me a dictator, but do you realize that in the years after the Chaco War we had *eight* presidents? Or was it nine? That isn't democracy; it's chaos." Stroessner's

figures were a little off, but his point was well taken.

Since 1962, there has in any case been a gradual political relaxation. Furthermore, Stroessner's regime has never been as oppressive as its opponents claim. If the recognized leaders of the opposition are in exile, Stroessner can say in his own defense, "After all, they *have* announced they want to kill me." And members of an opposition party still in Asunción have recently proclaimed that "We are now on the road toward democracy. The authorities respect the opposition; they allow us to have our offices up and down the country and to cooperate in the compilation of the electoral register; we can hold public meetings, fly our party flags and have music. Our newspapers, too, are now free to circulate." Although the leaders in exile refused to accept all this and considered their home-based party members as dupes or quislings, there does seem a chance that at last the 1.75 million people of Paraguay may enjoy the internal and external peace that has so long eluded them.

PROSPERITY is another matter. The two most widely grown crops are cultivated mainly for local consumption. These are cassava and maize, which, with meat, form the staple diet of the rural people. Paraguay's principal agricultural export is tobacco, most of which is sold in Argentina and Uruguay, and the country produces a high grade of cotton. The most valuable exports, however, are meat products and timber. Meat products and hides together brought the country almost $10 million in 1962. The traditional crop of yerba maté, or Paraguayan tea, continues to be exported, mostly to the other River Plate countries, and the brand most widely advertised in Buenos Aires comes from Asunción. Another Paraguayan potion that is equally popular in Argentina and Uruguay is *caña*, a highly potent product of sugar cane. This, however, is less widely advertised, possibly because most of that which is "exported" is smuggled across the border.

None of these exports, unfortunately, has done much for the Paraguayan economy. The country suffers from a chronic lack of both roads and rail lines; only a tiny fraction of the land is tilled; and despite increased investment by such U.S. companies as Esso, plus U.S. bank loans for industrial development, the average per capita income in Paraguay remains only $100 a year. Further, the country has generally been weakened by the number of exiles who have fled Paraguay's dictatorships and settled elsewhere, mostly in Argentina.

The only fuels Paraguay produces for its own use are charcoal and wood. Coal is nonexistent and expensive to import. The suspected oil deposits have never actually been found. Paraguay lacks the financial and technical means to engage in extensive exploration, and foreign oil companies have been reluctant to invest large sums in Paraguay in view of its history of periods of anarchy alternating with the kind of "strong" government most likely to nationalize foreign concerns once they have done the spadework. Therefore, oil, too, must be imported, and at considerable cost.

Of the hardwoods, the most important is quebracho, which comes from a dead-straight tree of up to 70 feet tall. Quebracho wood produces tannin, valuable in tanning leather, and is almost indestructible. Remarking that quebracho trees resemble nothing known in North America, a United States Minister to Paraguay, C. A. Washburn, said of them in 1871: "They are of very fine texture, and so heavy as to sink in water like iron. They are exceedingly hard to cut and work, and take a beautiful polish. But the greatest value of the wood consists in its durability. No kind of exposure seems to affect it. Sills of houses that have been exposed on one side to sun and rain, on another to the ground . . . still appear to be as sound as when first put in their places, three hundred years ago. For railroad ties they must be superior to anything else known." Quebracho wood is still used for railroad ties and telegraph poles in the River Plate area, but for construction it has lost ground to more modern substances such as steel and concrete.

WITH their lack of transport and paucity of obtainable natural resources, and with their turbulent and often tragic history, one might expect the Paraguayans to be a dour or doleful people. In fact, they are nothing of the sort, being gay and extremely sociable. The Calle Palma, the principal street of Asunción, while lacking any architectural pretensions, has a cheerful air, with brightly dressed girls whose laughter seems to show they are not worrying unduly about their possible superfluity.

The relative sparsity of automobile traffic makes Paraguayan cities seem more friendly; people stop and talk in groups outside cigarette kiosks or cafés, and in the stores the clerks have an unhurried politeness. The prevalence of the soft Guarani tongue, in both town and country, is a pleasant contrast to the stridency of much River Plate Spanish.

Even the nation's militant past somehow fits into a peculiarly Paraguayan pattern. There are monuments and war memorials everywhere, but the flags and wreaths which bedeck them have a proud rather than a tragic look. Military bands always seem to be playing somewhere, but they carry no overtones of menace, although in fact Paraguay still has a far larger Army than it can afford, and the Army still has the power to make or break governments.

PERHAPS the best guarantee that the Paraguayans may one day enjoy the stability and happiness they deserve is their extraordinary homogeneity. This is marked not only by their successful fusion of two different races—Guarani and Spanish—though that is unusual enough. It is shown also by a relative lack of class-consciousness that is hard to find in many more outwardly democratic nations. Finally, there is no dangerous gap between the very rich and the very poor. This unusual situation is partly the result of the fact that while Paraguay may produce enough to feed and clothe most of its people, thus avoiding extreme poverty, it does not possess the resources to attract would-be millionaires. At the same time, this social equality is historic. The Guarani Indians had no important divisions among them, and though the Spaniards introduced a social hierarchy during the colonial period, it did not suit the easygoing Paraguayan temperament. In contrast to countries like Peru, where there is a marked division of language and culture between Europeans and Indians, nearly all Paraguayans are mestizos and virtually all of them are bilingual. Only 40,000 people are classified as "pure" Indians, and with the exception of the more recent immigrant families, there are almost no "pure" whites. In Paraguay two peoples have merged to become one nation—an aspiration in many other countries but a reality in few.

Riding a high-wheeled, ox-drawn cart, the Paraguayan peasant family of Pedro Pablo Cáceres inches homeward along a dirt road.

A Land Still Too Backward to Reap Its Riches

Paraguay is the have-not nation of the River Plate area. Though endowed with rich farmland in the east and forests of valuable quebracho wood in the west, it remains sparsely populated and poor. The 1.8 million people are mostly undernourished and illiterate peasants. A scant 1 per cent of the countryside is cultivated, often by the most primitive methods —as it is by the Cáceres family *(shown above and on the following pages)*. Transportation is hampered by rutted dirt roads and a decrepit railway system. But the Government is trying to build roads, develop new farmland and attract new capital for industry.

PLOWING THE RICH SOIL, Paraguayan farmer Pedro Pablo Cáceres guides his wooden plow *(left)* behind a straining ox as his wife sows seeds by hand. The family owns one acre, on which it grows cassava, a starchy root, and thatch for roofing.

BINDING SHEAVES, Cáceres readies thatch *(opposite)* for the trip to market in his wagon. About 70 per cent of Paraguay's people are engaged in agriculture, most of them squatters on small, though fertile, forest clearings of less than 10 acres.

RESTING IN THE EVENING, Cáceres and his family *(below)* sit outside their one-room clay house in eastern Paraguay. At the left, Cáceres' aunt strums a ukulele. They own a few chickens and pigs, which wander freely in and out of the dwelling.

GUARANI INDIANS living in the Chaco are the poorest of all Paraguayans

A PROUD FAMILY of Guarani Indians stands outside its unwalled shelter on a ranch in the Chaco. About 40,000 pure-blooded Guarani are left in Paraguay: some are nomads who own virtually nothing and, like their ancestors, hunt game with bows and arrows. However, the recently completed Trans-Chaco Highway will give them a life line to the outside world.

VARIED EXPORTS of Paraguay, *potentially of great value, are still produced by primitive methods*

SPIDER-WEB LACE is patiently stitched *(above)* by a woman in the village of Itauguá, near Asunción. Itauguá lace is world-famous for its delicacy: some items take five years to complete.

YERBA MATE LEAVES, carried in huge sacks by pickers *(opposite),* are grown in rainy eastern Paraguay. The leaves brew a tea drink popular throughout the River Plate area.

QUEBRACHO WOOD is hauled out of the Chaco *(right)* on a train pulled by an ancient locomotive. Workers have to sprinkle sand on the tracks to prevent the wheels from slipping.

An angry mob carrying banners demanding the return of the exiled dictator Juan Perón closes in on mounted troops in the Argentine ci

Argentina's Search for Order

6

f Córdoba. The riot, which occurred during the 1964 visit of France's Charles de Gaulle, was quelled by the police with guns and tear gas.

OVER the whole of Argentina today hangs the shadow of the man who was removed from control in 1955—Juan Domingo Perón. The changes between Argentina today and the Argentina of the inter-World War years all came about shortly before and during the 10-year presidency of that one man, for good or for ill.

Before Perón, Argentina was on the surface a smug, prosperous and aristocratic society, featuring in its Cabinets, foreign embassies and other bastions of the "Establishment" the same names that had been there 50, 60 or more than 100 years ago: Alvear, Anchorena, Avellaneda, O'Farrell, Lavalle, Le Breton, Roca, Uriburu, Zárate—the descendants of the old landowners intermarried with the new immigrant plutocracy of the late 19th Century.

These names still appear in the glossy society magazines and the rotogravure section of the Sunday *La Prensa;* their present owners are pictured playing tennis at Hurlingham, sun-bathing at Mar del Plata,

89

skiing at Bariloche and sitting on ornate staircases at debutante dances. But despite the fact that many of them remain wealthy and wield power in the Argentine business community, they have lost much of their long-held political power and have in some ways become as irrelevant to the national scene as have the Boston Brahmins in the United States. And with their power have gone many of their prerogatives. In the big stores of Buenos Aires, the old families, instead of the onetime subservience, now get the same offhand treatment as anyone else. Their trips to Europe, once of annual regularity, are now curtailed by exchange restrictions. Their citadel, the stately Jockey Club in smart Calle Florida, was burned down in 1953 by Peronistas while the firemen concentrated on saving the neighboring buildings, and it has not yet been rebuilt. But they still have more money than most people and carry on their social charade in a make-believe world.

THE suburban and provincial middle class is not in such a happy position. These people never had the power or influence of the aristocracy, but in the old days they did enjoy a comfortable and secure existence, a prosperity that looked as if it would always continue to increase with the progress of the country. In a way they had the advantages of living simultaneously in the Edwardian era and the 20th Century—maidservants, cheap labor, deference and status without effort on the one hand; automobiles, radios, telephones and refrigerators on the other.

They still enjoy these 20th Century benefits, but so do the workers, and this seems to annoy some middle-class Argentines more than if they had lost them themselves. "What can you expect, *ché*," one woman remarked, "now that they've all got *television?*" She did not mean by this that the lower classes were now more apt to man the barricades, since the contrary is more likely to be true, but that they would become more *atrevido* (impertinent) and less willing to work long hours for nothing.

Only a few members of the middle class, of course, take quite such a Marie Antoinette view of the situation, but the rest have more legitimate grievances. Under Perón they were lumped together with the aristocrats as "oligarchs" in official oratory, were heavily squeezed by taxation and virtual blackmail

for Perón's extravagant and showy schemes for the workers, and were never sure whether the janitor, the maid, the local grocer or the train conductor might not be a Peronista agent ready to report their slightest criticism of the regime. After 1955, when Perón was overthrown, they expected a return to the status quo ante. Instead, thanks to the aftereffects of Perón's reckless fiscal program, they have found things getting financially tighter and tighter; and they have had little faith in the ability of the post-Perón governments.

ALL this they tie up with more generalized grumbles: the postal and telegraph services are deteriorating; the once-proud railroads are now dirty and unreliable; the paving stones taken up for cable repairs in many avenues of Buenos Aires are replaced with rubble; everything looks shabby—as indeed it does. A U.S. journalist, exaggerating somewhat, described Buenos Aires in 1961 as "looking like Warsaw or Prague."

It might be expected that at least the workers of Argentina, the beneficiaries of Perón's reforms, would be content, but they are not. A large majority of them actively supported Perón and therefore regarded the 1955 revolution as a return to the bad old days. Like the other classes, they have financial complaints; they also suffer from the effects of inflation, and they refuse to listen to the explanation that Perón's fiscal policy is the basic cause of it: *that* they regard as a disingenuous excuse by the bosses, and they continue to press for higher wages —which result in still higher prices.

How did the rule of Perón, which has left such a troubled and divided country behind it, come about? Partly it was the result of the century-old conservative rule of the landowning class. In spite of universal male suffrage and the election as President of the Radical politician Hipólito Irigoyen as far back as 1916, Argentina had remained socially stratified, and in fact had become *more* stratified since the more socially mobile days of colonization and immigration. The effect of this on an increasingly literate and politically aware working class was expressed with brutal candor by Perón's working-class wife Eva Duarte in her autobiography, *La Razón de Mi Vida (The Meaning of My Life)*: "In my heart I have found a fundamental emotion which . . . totally dominates my spirit and my life: this emotion is my *indignation in the face of injustice* [her italics]. Ever since I can remember, each injustice has made my soul suffer as if someone had driven a nail through it. From every age I retain the memory of some injustice which roused me to rebellion, and tore me apart inside. I very well remember being sad for several days when I found out that there were rich and poor in the world; and the strange thing is that I was not so upset by the existence of the poor as by the realization that at the same time there were the rich."

She and others like her had reason for their indignation. The promise heralded by the electoral reform of 1912 and the victory of the Radicals in 1916 had not been fulfilled. The Radicals, once in office, ran the country as autocratically as had the oligarchs before them and failed to make any fundamental changes in either the economic or social structure. They became so "respectable" that in the 1922 elections the Radical candidate was a wealthy aristocrat, Marcelo T. de Alvear (Irigoyen could not constitutionally succeed himself). Alvear was elected, with Irigoyen's backing, but when he refused to act as Irigoyen's puppet, a split developed in the Radical Party and the enemies of Irigoyen hived off to form a new group, which called itself the Antipersonalist Radicals.

This split weakened the Radical Party and bogged it down in internal dissension, so that it did not have the power to further its already vague progressive policies and they turned into a kind of generalized liberalism. This was no help to people like Eva Perón, who only differed from millions of her underprivileged compatriots in her articulateness and her determined character.

The Antipersonalist Radicals joined with the Conservatives to fight the 1928 elections, but the main

---

PRESIDENT IRIGOYEN'S ERA

The Argentine electoral reforms of 1912, which guaranteed universal male suffrage, gave the middle class and the workers their first chance to wrest control of their Government from the oligarchy—families of wealth and power. The people's choice was Hipólito Irigoyen, longtime head of the Radical Party, who became President in 1916 at the age of 66. A fierce idealist, Irigoyen kept his door open at all times to the workers, lived in a run-down house and gave his money to the poor. Unfortunately, Irigoyen was ill-educated, arrogant and had no conception of economics. He demanded blind loyalty from his subordinates—and appointed such dishonest ones that graft and corruption became the rule in Buenos Aires Government circles. Letters from foreign governments and vital legislative bills piled up unread on Irigoyen's desk. His second term was even more catastrophic than his first, and the Army toppled him in 1930.

---

body of the Radical Party retained enough strength to elect Irigoyen, after his mandatory absence from office, to a second term as President. But though eligible, he was no longer capable of carrying out the duties of the presidency. Almost senile at 76, he had become stubborn and would listen to nobody except sycophants who plundered the public purse, so that when the Wall Street crash reverberated around the world, Argentina, for all its natural wealth, found itself with an empty treasury. In 1930, for the first time in modern Argentine history, the Army stepped in and assumed control.

The role of the Army in the River Plate will be discussed in a later chapter, but one can mention now that its stance until very recently has been generally reactionary. So thoroughly corrupt and incompetent had Irigoyen's Government become, however, that Argentines of all classes welcomed the 1930 take-over by General José Félix Uriburu and turned bitterly against their old hero. Irigoyen himself had never joined in his colleagues' peculations, of which he was probably unaware, and he continued to live simply, but this did not save him from public wrath. A Buenos Aires mob invaded his unpretentious home and threw his belongings out of the window, including his iron bedstead and his chamber pot.

Uriburu stepped down and a presidential election was held in 1931. But the Radical candidate was disqualified by a ruling of the Army, and the main body of the Radicals consequently abstained from voting, alleging corrupt electoral practices. This left only two "progressive" parties. One was the Progressive Democrats, whose chief strength lay in the Province of Santa Fe. The other was the Socialist Party. These two groups combined in support of Lisandro de la Torre in the 1931 election, but they could not muster enough votes and whatever chance for real reforms there might have been was lost.

The Conservatives (who represented the more right-wing landowners), forming a coalition with the Antipersonalist Radicals and the Independent Socialists, gained a majority and held power until the Army coup of 1943, producing one popular and effective President in the process, Roberto M. Ortiz. He, however, became gravely ill with diabetes in 1940 and was succeeded by his Vice President, a colorless provincial lawyer named Ramón S. Castillo, who has been described as "a cross between Pétain and Neville Chamberlain." It was Castillo, and not Ortiz, who was eventually unseated by the Army.

THE coup of 1943 met with little popular support, but no opposition either. The Argentine people were tired of politicians, worried by a Government that seemed to have no views about World War II (most Argentines, contrary to popular foreign belief, were thoroughly pro-Allied), exasperated with the pettifogging pedantry of Castillo, and at the same time nagged by the feeling that two Army coups in 13 years, 1930 and then 1943, put their nation on the level of a "banana republic." The general attitude was one of helplessness and apathy. There was some scattered clapping as a celebrated regiment, the Granaderos a Caballo, founded by the liberator San Martín, clattered down Calle Corrientes, but there was bitter laughter when a dour bystander remarked: *"Andan a contramano"* (They're going the wrong way down a one-way street).

So they were. And so was the interim military Government that they ushered in. It was composed of members of a military lodge, on the lines of those of independence days, called GOU, standing (as its members intended) for either "Grupo de Oficiales Unidos" (United Officers Group) or "Gobierno, Orden, Unidad" (Government, Order, Unity). But the GOU produced little of either order or unity. Its first President, General Arturo Rawson, lasted one day and was then promptly appointed Ambassador to Brazil. His successors, Generals Pedro P. Ramírez and Edelmiro J. Farrell, were stolid soldiers with little knowledge of anything nonmilitary. Congress was dissolved. Army-style red tape

proliferated. The state radio's morning news bulletins became known as "The Orders of the Day."

Only once did one of the GOU leaders have the chance to demonstrate his soldierly training in a proper setting. On January 15, 1944, an earthquake hit the city of San Juan. President Ramírez hurried to San Juan to assure the population of the Government's support. Just as he was preparing to speak in the main plaza, there came another tremor. The crowd showed understandable signs of panic. Ramírez gestured to the band, which struck up the national anthem: *"Oíd, mortales, el grito sagrado. . . ."* The crowd responded: *"Libertad, libertad, libertad!"* The tremor subsided and no one was hurt. This show of courage and composure is a tribute to the Argentine people and to Ramírez as well.

As it happened, however, the major share of the publicity from the earthquake focused on an Army colonel named Juan Perón. A member of the GOU, Perón in 1943 might have been given a portfolio in the Cabinet, but he was distrusted by many of his fellow officers. Instead he got an apparently innocuous non-Cabinet post as president of the Department of Labor, a position which in his hands was to prove an invaluable springboard to power.

IN this capacity he took over the collection of aid for San Juan. His mistress at that time (he was then a widower) was a movie bit-player named Eva Duarte, who had recently become a success on Radio Belgrano. Together they drummed up aid for San Juan, putting up an enormous thermometer in Buenos Aires and demanding funds from businessmen. Perón's opponents, seeing the use that he was making of the San Juan disaster, nicknamed him *"el dueño del terremoto"* (the owner of the earthquake).

But Perón and Evita, as she was popularly known, had made their hit with most of the populace. And Perón had also used his official position to develop the country's weak and ill-organized unions into a nationwide trade-union movement under the banner of Confederación General del Trabajo. The workers, delighted at last to have some real power, became (and have remained) the principal supporters of Perón.

Finally the Army generals realized that they had in Perón a formidably large cuckoo in their GOU nest. On October 9, 1945, they removed him from all his posts, which by then included the vice-presidency. On October 10 Perón, in defiance of the GOU, appealed to the workers for support. A few days later he was shipped to the naval base of Martín García, between Argentina and Uruguay. But it was too late to stem the tide, if it had ever been possible. Evita rallied the newly aroused trade-unionists, who marched menacingly in torchlight procession from all parts of the city on Government House, demanding the return of Perón.

A frightened Government gave in and brought Perón to Buenos Aires. On October 17 a vast crowd gathered outside Government House in the Plaza de Mayo and for blocks up the surrounding streets to hear from General Farrell that Perón was free. But they did not want to hear from General Farrell. "We want Perón!" they yelled. The general, on the balcony, turned to an aide and muttered *"Esa gentuza porqué no se calla?"* (Why doesn't this rabble pipe down?). The words went out over the radio but, happily for the general, were inaudible to the crowd in the plaza.

Perón exercised the traditional Latin American assertion of power by keeping everybody waiting, then appeared to a thunderous roar of "Pe-RON! Pe-RON! Pe-RON!" In a powerful speech he announced himself as a candidate for the presidency, and at the end declared that he wanted to clasp to his bosom all those who earned their bread by the sweat of their brow. The next day his union, the CGT, declared a general strike, and truckloads of youths toured the city to smash up stores and newspaper offices.

ELECTIONS were set for February 1946. The Conservatives (currently calling themselves the National Democrats) lost heart and told their supporters and prospective candidates to make up their own minds. The remaining parties—the main body of the divided Radicals, the Socialists, the Progressive Democrats and the Communists—formed an electoral pact and fought under the banner of the "Unión Democrática." But they were no match for Perón. The Radicals insisted that a pair of their men, two party wheel horses disastrously named Tamborini and Mosca (the Tambourine and the Fly),

be made the coalition's candidates for president and vice president. Their campaign train was stoned and set on fire, and their meetings were broken up by Peronista bullyboys.

All this might have backfired in the polling booth, but at the beginning of February, the United States Department of State, with the approval of ex-Ambassador Spruille Braden, issued a Blue Book on Argentine relations with the Axis and criticizing Perón. Immediately, all over the country appeared posters of the kind used to announce soccer matches giving simply the election date and the words "PERON or BRADEN." The Fly and the Tambourine were contemptuously brushed aside. Perón, addressing a crowd of 120,000 in Buenos Aires, accused Braden of interference in Argentine affairs, denounced him as the organizer of a spy ring covering Latin America, and asserted that he had financed the Unión Democrática campaign with money "extorted from Argentine businessmen."

The voting on February 24 gave Perón only a small majority of the popular vote, but the electoral college overwhelmingly awarded him the presidency, and his followers gained about two thirds of the seats in the Chamber of Deputies, all but two of the seats in the Senate and all of the provincial governorships.

THE curious mixture of socialism, nationalism and plain old-fashioned dictatorship that characterized Perón's rule (partly from the need to keep his heterogeneous party together) is shown by a swift résumé of the Government's main actions in its first five years of power.

The first steps were taken even before Perón officially took over in June. On March 25, 1946, the Central Bank was nationalized, and on April 4 the privately owned grain elevators were expropriated. In May 1946, Perón took over the universities and by the end of the year had dismissed 70 per cent of their faculties. On June 1 an ordinance calling for registration of all religious bodies was passed.

After his inauguration, Perón's first major policy decision was to establish diplomatic relations with the Soviet Union. Subsequent significant events in the course of the year were the suspension of an opposition congressman for "disorderly conduct in the exercise of his functions," a law to nationalize the United River Plate Telephone Company and the British-owned gas companies, the nationalization of French-owned railroads, and the passing of the "Aguinaldo law," giving all Government workers a bonus of a month's pay at Christmas.

Perón started 1947 by proclaiming, on January 1, the First Five Year Plan for industrialization and a rag bag of other purposes. In April all but one of the members of the Supreme Court were dismissed and replaced by Peronistas; this was followed several months later by a thorough purge of the entire judiciary. In September the vote was granted to women, in the hope that they would gratefully cast it for Perón. On March 1, 1948, the Government bought and nationalized the huge British-owned railroad network, embodying Argentina's four most vital rail systems. In March of the following year a new Constitution was promulgated, allowing a president to be indefinitely re-elected. In July 1949, the ruling party, which had been called the Partido Laborista, was more realistically renamed the Partido Peronista. In August a Congressional committee on un-Argentine activities was set up, its real purpose being to eliminate domestic opposition.

IN January 1950 the Government started to close opposition newspapers, culminating a year later with the closure and expropriation of *La Prensa*, the principal Argentine daily and one of the great Spanish-language newspapers. In August of 1951, however, Perón made a serious error. A council of Peronistas approved Eva Perón as the vice-presidential candidate for the next elections. The Army would not stand for this, and under strong pressure Eva Perón withdrew her candidacy. This was the first real defeat the regime had suffered, and from then on, despite the bands and the banners and the mass rallies and the incessant propaganda, Perón's opponents began to take heart. The decline continued and accelerated during the next year, when the entire Argentine economy began to collapse.

Evita Perón, the girl from the wrong side of the tracks, the workers' darling, had been built up during Perón's years of rule into something like a living Madonna. To the scandal of many Catholics, she had been given the title of *Jefa Espiritual de la*

Nación—"Spiritual Chief of the Nation"—and her portrait had been placed on postage stamps. She had taken over all charitable works in the country under the guise of the Fundación Eva Perón, an all-purpose beneficent institution to which firms were forced to contribute "voluntary" donations, and which kept no books and published no accounts. She had made a quasi-regal progress through France, Spain and Italy in 1947, receiving from General Franco the Order of Isabél La Católica. She had caused wry amusement in the U.S. State Department by sending donations of used clothing for the poor of Washington, D.C.

All of this was fairly harmless. But in her bid for the vice-presidency she had overreached herself. A vice president may become a president, and a president is commander in chief of the armed forces. The Argentine Army *might* have accepted a woman of the caliber of Eleanor Roosevelt but not, as one colonel indignantly put it, *"una puta de los bajos fondos"* (a whore from the lower depths).

He need not have worried. Unknown to all but a few, Eva was a very sick woman. Her husband naturally won handily in the elections of November 1951, but the old panache had gone, the Movement (as Peronistas called the party) had gone sour, and on July 26, 1952, the announcement came that Evita had died—undoubtedly of cancer, though there were other rumors, including a ghoulish one that she had in fact died some time before and her death had been kept a secret.

HER death was the signal for the most macabre orgy of national mourning in modern times. Street lamps were draped in black. Bars were shut. Places of public entertainment were closed for a week. Hysterical women crawled around and around the presidential mansion on their knees, wailing and shrieking. But the Argentine people do not give their allegiance to ghosts: although her husband's name is still one to conjure with, Evita herself is today hardly ever mentioned.

After her death, Perón seemed to lose his grip on power. In 1955 the armed forces plucked up courage to begin planning for the removal of their former comrade in arms. The Church, which had for a long time put up with abuse from Perón, became belatedly outspoken against him. The business community and the sorely tried middle classes became overtly instead of covertly restive. On September 20, 1955, all these dissident groups, spearheaded by the Army, moved against Perón. When the news reached him that rebel troops had taken over in the provinces, he fled. If Eva had been alive he might have had the courage to make a stand. As it was he went, ironically for a leader of the workers, to Paraguay, to Venezuela, then to the Dominican Republic and finally to Spain—all at the time ruled by right-wing dictatorships. As for the memory of the Spiritual Chief of the Nation, Perón has since remarried and is wanted by the police in Argentina on a charge of having had sexual relations with a girl under the age of consent. A movement which was in part based on real social grievances and patriotic sentiments has left a shabby, squalid memory behind.

The trouble is that those who overthrew Peronismo, "all honourable men," have not found anything satisfactory to put in its place. Argentina today is a ship without a rudder. This uncertainty has reigned not only in the political but also in the economic and social fields, all of which are of necessity closely linked.

The first provisional President after Perón's fall, General Eduardo Lonardi, was a devout Catholic whose greatest belief was in "reuniting the Argentine family." This led to charges from his more militant colleagues that he was being soft on the Peronistas, and in November 1955 he was forced to resign. He was replaced by General Pedro Aramburu, who said that his job was merely to keep the country going until elections could be held. In his belief that the military should step down in favor of civilian government, he showed better sense than many military men, but it was a most unfortunate moment for

Argentina to have a regime pledged to inactivity.

Elections were held in February 1958. The two principal candidates, a pair of lawyers, were both Radicals who had run against Perón in 1951— Ricardo Balbín and Arturo Frondizi. But once again the Radicals had split: Balbín stood as a People's Radical, paradoxically representing the middle class, and Frondizi as an Intransigent Radical in the Irigoyen tradition. Balbín repudiated Perón, if not all of his reforms. Frondizi wooed the Peronista vote, promising that all the "social benefits" of Peronismo—higher wages, generous pensions and so on—would be retained, while somehow the country's sick economy would be cured. How all this was to be brought about was another matter. The social benefits achieved under Perón, like the "prestige" purchase of transatlantic liners and the inauguration of an unprofitable airline, had been financed basically by drawing on the country's capital resources rather than from current income. Worse, Perón's insistence on industrialization and his neglect of agriculture had cut into the country's principal and essential export, beef, as well as other agricultural products. These, though most workers did not realize it, were the causes of Argentina's economic difficulties. It was widely alleged then and afterward that Frondizi had signed a secret agreement with Perón and that the Peronistas (whose party was ineligible) had been told by their founder to vote the Frondizi ticket.

Among the many candidates with their competing promises, there was one lone, warning voice, the economist Alvaro Alsogaray. He promised, in effect, toil, tears and sweat, though not blood—and he got less than 1 per cent of the vote. Frondizi romped handsomely home, and his troubles had begun.

Few heads of government can have ridden out so many crises. As soon as he was inaugurated in May

---

EVITA—SAINT OF THE WORKERS

Eva Duarte de Perón was born out of wedlock in 1919 in a small Pampa village. At the age of 24 she went to Buenos Aires, where she met Colonel Juan Perón at a party, became his mistress and was soon working to further his campaign for the presidency. Her speechmaking ability and attractiveness endeared her to Argentina's working class and to the women voters. Perón put her in charge of all health and labor programs. She set up the Eva Perón Foundation to which business, government and labor donated an estimated $100 million a year. Evita, as she was called, spent vast sums on hotels for working girls, children's villages and homes for the aged. During some public appearances, she would give away fistfuls of 100-peso notes. Although Evita lavished money on herself, the workers remained convinced that she was a saintly benefactress, and when she died at the age of 33, they called for her canonization.

1958, Frondizi had to announce a probable deficit of $1.2 billion, an adverse balance of payments and a drop in gold reserves. The situation was so bad, with soaring inflation and falling production, that presently Frondizi called in his erstwhile opponent Alsogaray to take over the economy. He followed this by declaring two meatless days each week so that there might be enough beef for export.

Frondizi's period in office was from the first beset by labor troubles. Workers saw their real wages dropping behind the cost of living and felt that the Intransigent Radicals had betrayed their electoral promises, and in 1958 and 1959 there were serious strikes on the railroads and in the meat-packing and oil industries. Metalworkers, glassworkers and textile workers walked out in 1959, as did banking and insurance clerks. Several general strikes also broke out in that same year.

BETWEEN the years 1958 and 1962, there was ever-increasing tension within the political parties and between the parties and the armed forces; there were constant resignations and Cabinet reshuffles. By the beginning of 1960, however, it did seem as if Frondizi's Government might be out of the woods. The oil industry in particular was booming, and the worst political unrest seemed to have faded. The newspapers, in Argentina and abroad, began to publish articles with titles like "Argentina Turns the Corner." The Argentine people were unhappy with austerity and forced the dismissal of Alsogaray, but his replacement by the respected Roberto Alemann seemed to promise continuity.

Then, on March 18, 1962, came the shock.

Feeling that it was now safe to do so, Frondizi for the first time allowed Peronistas to run for office. Ten of the 14 provinces with gubernatorial races returned Peronista pluralities. The Peronistas won 44 of the 86 seats at stake in Congress, and they even won control of the Province of Buenos Aires.

There was not, even at that "moment of truth," much real fear that Perón himself would return. That would have meant civil war, for which the ex-dictator was known to have no stomach. Nor were the Peronista leaders themselves all that keen to have him back: they had tasted independent power and they enjoyed its savor. What frightened most

non-Peronistas was that power would pass into the hands of politically irresponsible people, mostly Perón-trained labor leaders, whose only experience had been that of demanding ever-higher wages. Others feared a proletarian dictatorship, while still others foresaw sheer chaos. Liberal Argentines asked themselves the historic question: what do you do when the voters democratically choose a nondemocratic government? For this would have been the almost inevitable result.

Frondizi refused to resign, and the armed forces, which might have acted, stayed their hand partly through fear of world opinion and partly because they simply did not know what to do. But finally they came to a decision and on March 30 bundled Frondizi aboard an aircraft bound for Martín García, the River Plate island where, ironically, Perón had spent his 1945 exile. They had answered the question the easy way: you get rid of anti-democrats—the Peronistas—by acting undemocratically.

There followed more than a year of political bumbledom. While most Argentines, willy-nilly, continued to go to their jobs, bring up their children and hope for the best while prophesying the worst, the Government installed by the military limped and spluttered through a series of crises that must have made Frondizi, in comfortable exile, look at the daily papers a little quizzically.

ON July 7, 1963, the interim Government honored its pledge to hold elections—without, of course, Peronista candidates. Dr. Arturo Illia, a country physician who was the candidate of the People's Radicals, won the presidency. Although he did not receive a popular majority, he had a large plurality, and a multiparty coalition of members of the electoral college banded together to elect him.

Illia owed his election mainly to the fact that he seemed the least controversial candidate. And, indeed, although no president, of Argentina or anywhere else, *can* completely avoid controversy, Illia's first announcements of his plans contained something that would appeal to almost every Argentine. In his inaugural speech, on October 12, he stated, among other things, that oil contracts signed with foreign firms by President Frondizi would be annulled, that the armed forces should get back to their job of guarding the nation's frontiers and leave government to those whose business it was, and that in foreign affairs Argentina should be nationalist and decidedly Latin American. At the same time, he said, Argentina should establish commercial relations with everybody who offered economic advantages. He also announced that there would be a "social truce" between employers and employees and that farm production would be spurred through a system of Government loans to farmers.

MANY of these aims could be counted on, of course, to displease some segments of Argentine public opinion and to please others. But soon Argentines began to criticize Dr. Illia, not for what he proposed to do, but for not doing anything at all. If there is such a thing as "divine discontent," the Argentines have it. They have a saying: "God is an Argentine"; this is not a claim to divinity but carries the unspoken corollary: "If He weren't we'd be even worse off than we are already."

In fact, the Argentines, in comparison with the rest of the world, are not all that badly off. They have another saying: "Argentina grew great in spite of her governments," and this would seem to be true. Argentina today boasts a comparatively comfortable standard of living; it normally consumes as much meat per capita as Australia or the United States, and the bulk of the people not only eat well but have decent homes and at least some of the mechanical conveniences of modern life. Some Argentines, like Eva Perón in her youth, remain very poor; and there are pockets of poverty in both town and camp, but as the world goes, Argentina bears a comparatively light burden. Nor does Argentina suffer, as so many nations do, from the problem of race. Argentine Indians look little different from Spaniards; Argentine Negroes are almost nonexistent. This is not to say that Argentines, as whites, have no race prejudice. They do, but mostly they have no chance or reason to show it.

. As a country, Argentina is far from poor, whatever its rate of exchange or its cost of living. Apart from its vast cattle ranches, its sheep farms in Patagonia, its grainfields and its new industries. it has its oil. Under President Frondizi, the Government signed agreements with foreign oil companies which allowed them to develop large areas of Argentina. Within three years, oil production tripled, some 660 miles of pipeline had been built, and Argentina was able to satisfy the needs of its own consumers and to export oil to other South American countries. President Illia's canceling of these agreements cut off the flow of foreign initiative and capital, but the Y.P.F.—Fiscal Petroleum Wells, a federal concern— shows signs of profiting from the foreign example. If U.S. and other oil companies were allowed back into Argentina, the country's oil industry would undoubtedly make a still larger contribution to the national economy. Whether Argentina, fearful of foreign economic domination, will allow this is another matter.

This fear is symptomatic, for Argentina is, in some respects, a schizophrenic nation. It is Latin American and proud of it—and thus in a way anti-North American. It is also European and proud of it—and thus in another way anti-North American. But above all it is Argentine, as Australia is Australian or Canada Canadian. It is a part of Europe transplanted to the Americas, but unlike some other countries, it is proud to admit it—and indeed to boast of it.

APART from the political activities of its armed forces, Argentina is Western European in its whole tradition. The Gaucho was a passing phase. Like Western Europe, it is affected by United States *mores;* like Western Europe, its feelings about them are very ambivalent. Some Argentines deplore the twist and Coca-Cola and talk as if these things were the sum total of U.S. culture, while at the same time they praise U.S. novels, poems and plays.

All this sounds as if Argentina has a strange mixture of prejudices. So, like most countries, it does. At the same time it is a country with its own deep feelings: it reveres its flag and its national anthem, its old military regiments and their flags, and the names of the battles in which it won independence. .It loves its highly idiosyncratic Spanish, its ugly old buildings, its British railroad stations. It almost loves the problems that it faces, because they are *Argentine* problems, which strangers (so Argentines feel) cannot really understand. To millions of people it is home, and most of them, whatever their grumbles, would not think of leaving.

RISING POLITICIAN, Juan Perón sits at the head of a table of shirt-sleeved friends at a party during his 1945 campaign for the presidency. Perón won the election by a huge margin.

The Rise and Fall
of a False Champion

Juan Domingo Perón installed and perpetuated his 10-year dictatorship by tapping a new source of Argentine political power: the workers. As head of the Department of Labor in 1943, he welded the nation's hitherto weak unions into a single strong labor movement. A mass labor demonstration in 1945 forced the country's military Government to allow Perón to run for the presidency. Although Perón's economic policies almost wrecked Argentina, many workers never understood why the economy was failing and have continued to hope for his return.

FLAMBOYANT DICTATOR, General Perón and an elegantly dressed Eva *(right)* say goodbye to their poodles as they leave the presidential mansion on their way to a reception in 1950.

ANXIOUS LEADER, Perón, with Eva beside him, seeks to bolster his power in 1952 by announcing his ailing wife's return to public life. Eva, however, died of cancer shortly thereafter.

MOURNING HUSBAND, a shaken Perón *(third from left)* marches to Eva's funeral. After the popular Eva's death, which provoked hysterical lamentation, Perón's enemies took heart.

ILLEGAL DEMONSTRATION by Roman Catholics on June 9, 1955, protests Perón's policies. When two Catholic leaders were exiled in retaliation, the Vatican excommunicated Perón.

IMPROVISED ALTAR in the Santo Domingo church is the setting for Mass *(below)* on June 26, 1955. Peronistas had sacked a dozen churches after the Catholic demonstration.

ANGRY MEETING of the old Radical Party *(above)* plans future moves during the lull after the Peronista attacks on the Church. Later the Radicals demanded a return of freedoms.

AROUSED MEMBERS of Perón's General Confederation of Labor *(below)* head for a rally on August 31, 1955, where a desperate Perón exhorted them to "annihilate" his opponents.

MOB VIOLENCE and protest rallies racked Buenos Aires in the months preceding Perón's departure in 1955

EXPLOSIVE CROWD in Plaza de Mayo on August 31 listens to Perón's call for death to his enemies and answers, "Hang them! Kill them!" But the Army rose against Perón 16 days later.

SURRENDERING to revolutionary soldiers in Córdoba, a Peronista police official waves a white flag *(above)*. Troops in the provinces started the revolt and the Navy then joined in.

ESCAPING, Perón *(fourth from left, below)* transfers from his first refuge, a Paraguayan gunboat *(background)*, to a seaplane which flew him to Paraguay. He eventually reached Spain.

BURNING PERON DOCUMENTS, a middle-class crowd destroys the contents of a Peronista meeting hall in Buenos Aires. The city surrendered on September 19, 1955, after the rebelling Navy had threatened bombardment. In the chaotic days that followed, mobs roamed the city, burning and looting. Perón himself managed to make his escape with upward of $50 million.

URUGUAYAN RANCH HAND shoos a flock of sheep into a corral with his poncho. Much of Uruguay is covered by a rolling plain—an extension of the Argentine Pampa. Uruguayans raise sheep primarily for their wool rather than meat.

7

Fashioning Uruguay's Modern State

URUGUAY has often been called the Switzerland of South America, largely because of its small size, democratic institutions and high standard of living. But the analogy cannot be stretched much further: Uruguay has no wrist-watch factories or mountains, and instead of four languages it boasts only one.

A nearer parallel is with New Zealand. Like New Zealand, Uruguay has more sheep than people and depends for its existence on the output of its ranches. Like New Zealand, too, Uruguay's trade for many years depended on British markets. And the attitude of Uruguayans toward neighboring Argentina is remarkably similar to the view that New Zealanders take of Australia. Both New Zealanders and Uruguayans tend to consider their larger neighbors too big and bumptious and, when abroad, object to being constantly taken for Australians and Argentines respectively.

But a third comparison, not often made, has also a certain validity—that with Sweden. As Sweden helped pioneer the welfare state in Europe, so Uruguay pioneered it in the Americas—indeed, the most right-wing Uruguayan politicians support policies that would be regarded as dangerously radical in the majority of American countries from Canada to Cape Horn. And, like the Swedes, the Uruguayans have a tendency to become bored with a too comfortable and too uneventful life. European refugees who entered Uruguay's ever-open doors, and who are now proud to call themselves Orientales—the old colonial term by which Uruguayans still like to describe themselves—begin after a time to complain that "nothing ever happens here," forgetting that the very reason they first sought Uruguayan sanctuary was that altogether too much was happening in the countries from which they came.

HOW Uruguay, from being an *enfant terrible* for most of the 19th Century, became a model of rectitude in the 20th is hard to say. The British historian Thomas Carlyle, who saw the march of events as due entirely to outstanding personalities, would have put it all down to one man: José Batlle y Ordóñez, the founder of the modern republic. Marxists would scoff at this posthumous cult of personality: in their view the causes of political change are always economic. Probably the answer is somewhere between the two. At the turn of the century, a country sick of civil strife found the man it needed to put an end to the disorder. As the caption beneath wartime portraits of Winston Churchill, which proliferated throughout Uruguay, put it, Batlle became *"El Hombre del Momento."*

José Batlle (pronounced *Ba´-zhay*) y Ordóñez was born in Montevideo in May 1856, at the height of the period of *caudillismo,* when the country's leaders were *caudillos,* or smalltime war lords. The son of a general who occupied the presidency from 1868 to 1872, Batlle had an unusually good education. After studying law at the University of the Republic in Montevideo, he went on to the Sorbonne, then as now the mecca of intellectual Rioplatenses. While he was in Paris, Batlle avidly studied philosophy and toyed with the idea of becoming a teacher.

On his return to Montevideo he instead became a political journalist. He fearlessly flayed the dictators who ruled turbulent Uruguay and the sordid state of the country's politics. Of one dictator, General Máximo Santos, he wrote: "The national sovereignty, honor, and dignity were crucified by his henchmen." On several occasions he was attacked in the streets, and he suffered temporary imprisonment. After eight years of writing for other men's

newspapers, he founded, in 1886, his own paper, *El Día,* still today the most authoritative (and quite the dullest) newspaper in Uruguay. Later he became a member of the legislature as Deputy for the Department of Salto and, after a series of political vicissitudes, became a Senator in 1898 and was elected to the presidency for the first time in 1903. The difference between this impeccably constitutional career and the Gaucho-style independence of the national hero Artigas, revered as the Father of the Nation, was symptomatic of the country's development during the 19th Century.

So was the policy Batlle initiated. He believed passionately that freedom and justice and equality were not just words, and he set out to make them realities for the Uruguayan people. One of his initial victories was a bill legalizing divorce (a very "liberal" measure in a Roman Catholic country), the first step in Batlle's long struggle to emancipate Uruguayan women. Also during his first term as President, Batlle inaugurated his drive to vastly expand and improve the country's educational system, and he succeeded in having the death penalty abolished. At the end of this term, he began a campaign, which was to last eight years, to push through laws calling for an eight-hour day. During his second term (1911-1915), he backed a staggering list of reforms, ranging from care for the aged to loans for farmers; all of these, like the eight-hour day, were considerably in advance of their time even by European standards, let alone by those of Latin America. In general he undertook to narrow the gap between rich and poor. "The gap must be narrowed," he said, "and it is the duty of the state to attempt that task."

THE basic principles behind Batlle's enlightened reforms were enshrined in the new Constitution of 1918. (Uruguay had had a Constitution since 1830, but until Batlle's era it had usually been honored in the breach.) More of Batlle's reforms found their way into subsequent Constitutions, but the foundations of Uruguay's "New Deal" were laid by Batlle before World War I, and most of the major reforms were enacted into law during Batlle's lifetime. After his death, in 1929, his faction of the Colorado Party, which had become the standard-bearer

106

of liberalism, continued to base its policy on Batlle's ideas. The more conservative Blanco Party did not seriously try to obstruct Colorado reforms. This was partly because the social climate of the country, conditioned by years of peace and relative prosperity, was favorable to liberal ideas: even the wealthy were not much alarmed by the steady but painless advance of social security, workers' rights, and an ever greater measure of social and economic equality. If the Blancos had dug in and resisted change, they would have suffered greater electoral defeats than they did.

Uruguay's democratic evolution was not without setbacks. A coup d'état in 1933 temporarily resulted in government by decree. A new Constitution in 1934 confused rather than improved the political scene, and it was not until 1942 that yet another Constitution fully restored Uruguay's political democracy. However, in its social and economic principles the 1934 Constitution continued along the liberal path. It codified most of Batlle's ideas in a single document and covered almost every aspect of Uruguayan life. From earlier Constitutions it took over such basic provisions as complete freedom of speech and the written word, the prohibition of arbitrary arrests, the abolition of the death penalty, a declaration that prisons were intended for reform rather than punishment, equality of all religions, and the separation of church and state. But it went much further, and in clear and specific terms it spelled out its practical clauses. For example, the exploitation of children in whatever way was prohibited; parents had the same obligations toward illegitimate offspring as legitimate ones; the state would take responsibility for the sick who could not afford private doctors; and social security laws would provide financial protection in cases of accident, illness or unemployment.

Many countries, including Latin American ones, have had equally admirable constitutions. The difference in the case of Uruguay is that this one—

URUGUAYAN STATESMAN, José Batlle y Ordóñez during two terms as President was responsible for making his country into a stable and prosperous democracy.

many of whose provisions were already on the statute books—was enforced and, with subsequent revisions in the same spirit, still is.

More than that. Although it is seldom used, there is a Constitutional provision that calls for referendums, or plebiscites, on the Swiss model, if the people demand them. Thus the people can have a direct voice in any proposals that specifically affect their lives.

Of course, to allow referendums is easier in Uruguay than in less compact and more heterogeneous communities. A Tass correspondent in the River Plate, twitted by a Russian ex-compatriot on the fact that such referendums did not take place in the Soviet Union, said, "We happen to have a larger country." He had a point. In modern terms, given the telegraph, the telephone, the bus and the train, not to mention radio and television, Uruguay, with a population of only 2.6 million, has the cohesion of a Greek city-state. Or at least Montevideo has this cohesion—and Montevideo has about one half of the people and most of the power, although the landowners of "the camp" have disputed this dominance for generations.

But despite these advantages, Uruguay has had its troubles. One problem in the first half of this century was that Batlle's Colorado Party, however internally divided, kept on winning every national election by a small majority and with monotonous regularity. This worried the Colorados almost as much as it did the principal opposition party, the Blancos. The Colorado majority was sometimes too small to govern effectively, and the Blancos, perpetually in a minority, sometimes resorted to obstructionist tactics.

So in 1951 a plebiscite was held submitting the text of a new Constitution to the electorate. The principal new provision of this Constitution was that the presidency would be replaced by a "collegium" to be called the National Council of Government, made up of nine members, six from the majority party and three from the principal minority party; such a change would guarantee the Blancos a voice in government. Members of the majority party would rotate the chairmanship each year for four years, at the end of which a new council would be elected by direct popular vote.

The electorate voted in favor of the changes— despite the fact that a similar system had been tried once before, from 1918 to 1933, and then abandoned—and the new Constitution went into effect in 1952. By an ironic twist of fate, in the elections held six years later the Blancos gained a majority, and the Colorados relinquished power for the first time in 93 years. The Colorados, who retained a voice in the council, thus benefited from a measure that was believed would benefit their opponents. The new Constitution had another advantage from the Colorado point of view since it carried to fruition Batlle's ambition to have the country governed by a collegium rather than by a single, strong president who, Batlle had always feared, might abuse his power. Unfortunately, the collegium system has not proved wholly efficient, and some Uruguayan politicians are calling for a return to a single chief executive.

IN fact, as Uruguayan politics operate today, it makes only a marginal difference which of the two major parties is in power. As has often happened with the Republican and Democratic Parties in the United States, there are more ideological divisions within the Colorado and Blanco Parties than there are between their respective electoral platforms. On the whole, as the party of Batlle, the Colorados have tended to appeal to the more progressive urban voters, while the Blancos have made their principal appeal to the more conservative "camp." But both parties are factionalized into groups supporting particular personalities, sectional interests or ideologies. In the 1962 elections, for example, the Blanco Party was split into such factions as the "orthodox" Herreristas (followers of a Rightist politician, the late Luis Alberto de Herrera), the Ruralists (whose name is self-explanatory), and the Unión Blanca Democrática, which was a middle-of-the-road group of urban orientation. Similar complex and shifting divisions have also been the rule in the Colorado Party.

Partly as the result of this internecine strife, and partly because of the ebullient Uruguayan personality, the country's politics are lively and outspoken. Political cartoons in the Montevideo newspapers are probably the most uninhibited in the Americas, and so sometimes are the legislators, who frequently and openly insult one another, often in earthy terms. Occasionally these impolite remarks, or some especially outspoken newspaper articles, lead to duels, which are still legal in Uruguay. Former President Luis Batlle Berres, a nephew of the reformer, was involved in several challenges and took sword in hand at least twice, seriously wounding one of his opponents. Fortunately, the country's system of voting, by which an unsuccessful candidate's votes can be transferred to a second choice of the same party, gives the resulting legislature more cohesion than might be expected.

URUGUAYAN politics are also spiced by the existence of a number of other parties besides the Blancos and Colorados. Although these groups are all highly vocal, their strength is limited. The Socialists have had the wind taken out of their sails by the Batllista reforms, which have implemented most of the policies for which Socialism traditionally stands. The Roman Catholics are represented by the Christian Democrat Party, which again makes small appeal because of the lack of religious controversy in Uruguay and the general lack of political militancy among Uruguayan Catholics.

The only remaining group of any importance is the Communist Party, but this, too, has had many of its policies and much of its appeal absorbed by the Colorados. During the 1940s, a Uruguayan Communist leader complained to the Soviet embassy in Montevideo (then as now one of the largest Soviet diplomatic missions in Latin America) that the embassy was paying less attention to his local Communists than to the Blancos and Colorados. He was told bluntly: "We have to deal with the people in power and those who are likely to get into power. You aren't." Perhaps the reason they were not and are not in power was best summed up in an article in a Montevideo paper headed "Have We a Middle Class?" The writer concluded that not only did Uruguay have one but almost everybody belonged to it.

Like every other country, Uruguay has its lunatic fringe, but apart from a small and mostly youthful neofascist group, whose inspiration comes from Argentina, it is harmless and often contributes to civic gaiety. The most engaging of these marginal groups was led by one Domingo Tortorelli, a prosperous vegetable merchant who ran in a postwar election as a self-appointed candidate simultaneously for senator, deputy, president and vice president. His platform and campaigning were refreshing if not wholly edifying. Tortorelli promised two fountains on every street corner in Montevideo, one fountain flowing with milk for children, the other with wine for adults. Montevideo, he said, should have a roof built over it to protect the people in rainy weather. He also advocated the construction of a superhighway from Montevideo to Colonia running downhill in both directions in order to save gasoline. His nightly speeches sometimes drew large crowds. The crowds often pelted him with vegetables, which he professed to like as being good for his business. Unfortunately for Tortorelli, however, he attracted more vegetables than votes.

THE Uruguayans do not, like some Latin Americans, take themselves very seriously. At the same time, they have an unusual self-confidence. On the occasion of a census in Montevideo, the Government asked for public cooperation in posters headed *"Cuántos somos? Cómo somos? Cómo vivimos?"* (How many are we? What are we? How do we live?). A revue was promptly put on at a theater with the same title, plus an added question: *"Porqué somos?"* (Why are we?). Only people who are sure of themselves would make such jokes. This maturity has given Uruguay, considering its size, a unique international prestige, both in Latin America and elsewhere. During World War II, when it never wavered in its adherence to the Allied cause, Uruguay's Foreign Minister, Dr. Alberto Guani, earned the nickname of *"El Canciller de las Américas"* (The Chancellor of the Americas) because of the weight he carried in inter-American diplomatic relations.

Despite its enlightened laws and general stability, Uruguay does have its measure of troubles, some of them caused by the country's very virtues. The civil service administering the welfare state is cumbrous and overstaffed: to combat the "spoils system," several laws were passed which stop incoming administrations from dismissing functionaries taken on by their predecessors—but fail to forbid them from taking on any more, with logical results. The trade-unions are so powerful and so militant for higher wages that paralyzing strikes are becoming a serious threat to the national economy. The benefits of the welfare state, legislated by townsmen, are still loaded in favor of the city, and indeed the agricultural sector on which the whole economy depends has tended to be neglected by governments sitting in Montevideo. Largely because of this neglect, the country has recently suffered from galloping inflation. Prices are high, and both the workers and the elderly, beneficiaries of the country's handsome welfare measures, stand by helplessly as the cost of living climbs beyond their means. The Uruguayan peso has been devalued, and the country's gold reserves have tumbled. Some dour prophets have said that the whole Uruguayan system is on trial—and may not survive.

But these are, hopefully, remediable evils, and the structure of the state remains sound. There is complete freedom of speech, press and association, and this in itself is a guarantee that abuses can be remedied. There is remarkably little religious bigotry, racial friction or class prejudice—certainly less than in the United States or Britain. The small Negro minority is still, it is true, mostly at the bottom of the economic ladder. But there is no question of discrimination in public places or even (noticeably, at any rate) in housing.

BUT what is truly remarkable about Uruguay is not the lack of bigotry but the positive spirit of equality. Writing more than 75 years ago in *The Purple Land,* W. H. Hudson perceived and praised this natural democracy: "Here the lord of many leagues of land and of herds unnumbered sits down to talk with the hired shepherd . . . and no class or caste difference divides them, no consciousness of their widely different positions chills the warm current of sympathy between two human hearts. . . . What a change to a person coming from lands with higher and lower classes, each with its innumerable hateful subdivisions. . . ." This egalitarian spirit is still alive in Uruguay today.

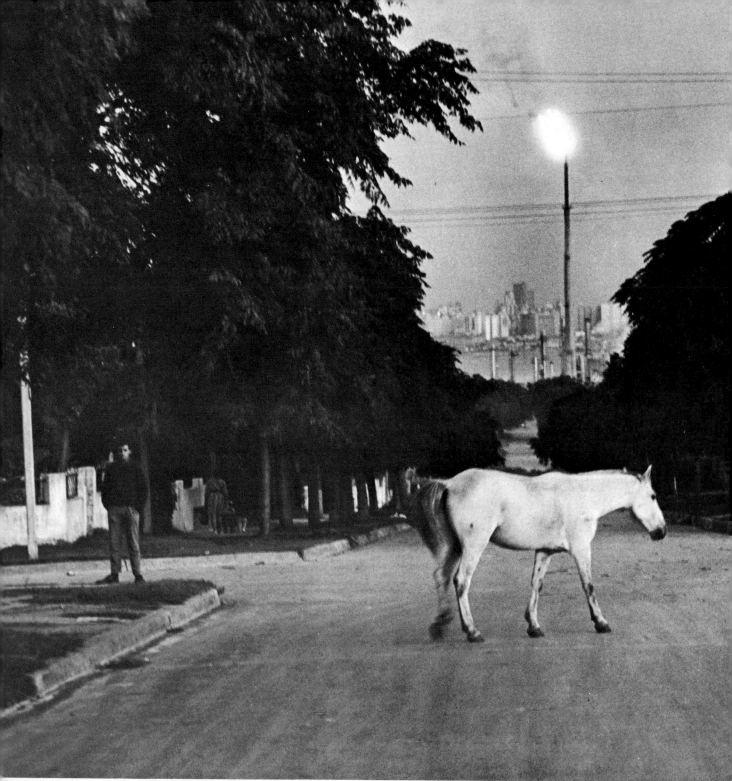

A horse wanders across a street in suburban Montevideo looking for forage. Horse owners in Uruguay often let their animals loose to nibble

Providing a Good Life
for a United People

Uruguay in many respects deserves its reputation as a model nation. Blessed with a gentle climate, fine grazing land, a homogeneous people and ease of communications, the country has in modern times augmented its good fortune with progressive laws.

shrubbery, as it is cheaper than buying fodder. Nobody seems to mind.

Today, free education, public housing, medical care and old-age pensions are provided for all. Problems do exist: inflation and an unwieldly bureaucracy have taken a toll. Yet, if changes must come, stable Uruguay will probably weather them safely.

RAKISH TIN LIZZIE stands parked outside a Montevideo factory *(above)*. High import duties have made cars extremely expensive in Uruguay, and the streets are full of antique models.

MODERN BUILDINGS overshadow Montevideo's older architectural landmarks, such as the turreted castle in the foreground. Montevideo holds about half of the nation's people.

VAST, PILLARED HALLWAY leads into Uruguay's impressive marble-and-granite Legislative Palace *(above)*, the meeting place since 1925 for the country's bicameral General Assembly.

TREASURED DOCUMENT, Uruguay's 1825 Declaration of Independence lies open in a glass case guarded by a sentry *(left)* in one of the halls of the Legislative Palace in Montevideo.

EXECUTIVE COUNCIL which replaced the one-man presidency in 1952 registers a vote in this rare photograph of a session. This nine-member council is elected every four years by popular vote; six of its members are drawn from the majority party and the other three from the minority. This form of executive guarantees the minority a voice in high policy decisions.

MEDICAL SERVICES in Uruguay
are excellent in quality,
inexpensive and available to all

RETARDED CHILDREN buy candy from a vendor outside their Government-operated school in Montevideo. A progressive institution, the school trains teachers from other countries.

CRIPPLED CHILDREN play outdoors during recess at the Franklin D. Roosevelt School *(below)*. Uruguay provides free schooling from the elementary through the university level.

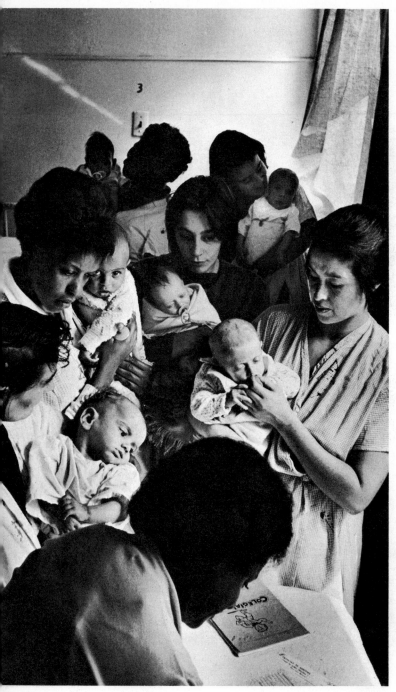

INTERESTED MOTHERS crowd around a nurse while they wait for examinations at Montevideo's Pereira Rosell Hospital for children, one of the largest medical centers in Latin America.

HUGE HOSPITAL of the national university in Montevideo, looming 22 stories high, is a major center of low-cost care, teaching and research. There are six large hospitals in the city, giving medical care free to all needy cases. Uruguay has more doctors per capita than any other Latin American nation. Many of them have received training in hospitals in the United States.

IN A CLASSROOM, law students listen to a lecture at Uruguay's national university. About 30 per cent of the university's students are enrolled in law and 20 per cent study medicine.

AT A CAFE, students and teachers gather for discussion or newspaper browsing *(above)*. Many Government employees are able to attend the university since they work only half days.

BETWEEN LECTURES, students *(right)* chat and read bulletins. Because higher education is free in Uruguay, the number of people trained for the professions exceeds the demand.

Paraguayan troops goose-step past Asunción's Government Palace during a parade celebrating the anniversary of the nation's independence.

In the 1930s the Paraguayan Army was trained by German officers.

Politics and Pressure Groups

THE pattern has been a familiar one among the "emerging" nations during the last decades. The colonial power moves out in response to the people's demands for freedom. But the people, largely untrained in the subtleties of self-government, do not know how to exercise their new freedom. The old colonial government is gone; the new one does not know how to grasp the reins of power. The result is a power vacuum, and into this void rush forces eager to seize control for themselves.

This is more or less what happened in the River Plate area after Spanish control was effectively thrown off in the early 19th Century. Theoretically, as in the United States, sovereignty was transferred to the people of the countries concerned. But the people, despite their admiration for the French and American Revolutions, had no experience in the operation of representative government aside from the *cabildos*, or town councils, which were made up of the local men of wealth and importance rather than of elected officials. As a result, the earliest governments in the River Plate tended to be juntas—groups of men

119

who simply took power. Even after constitutions were written, setting up representative governments with elected legislatures, neither the people nor the politicians seemed capable of running these governments smoothly. Almost incessant power struggles resulted in the breakdown of governmental processes and in the rule of juntas, triumvirates and dictators, many of them supported by the Army.

In addition to the Army, two other groups have had a strong voice in the affairs of Argentina, and to some extent in the affairs of the other River Plate nations. These two pressure groups have been the Roman Catholic Church and the landed interests. Sometimes these groups and the Army have been in conflict with one another; sometimes they have been in themselves divided on policy or ideology. But with varying success all three have continued to make their influence felt ever since independence. For more than a century and a half they have represented the "Establishment"—those with the controlling power —in the River Plate. In at least two of the republics, Argentina and Paraguay, one or more of them still form powerful lobbies, or pressure groups.

THE Army, especially in Paraguay and Argentina, has been convinced that it had the right to step in whenever it considered that the civilian government was heading for trouble. In a majority of cases these incursions by the Army have produced still more trouble, and when the military has actually taken over the government it has usually proved itself inept. Nevertheless, the Army has remained a powerful pressure group in these nations.

The Church has had far less power in the River Plate than it has had in other parts of South America. However, it has wielded considerable, if never crucial, influence on the side of conservatism. Also conservative have been the landowners, and the histories of Argentina and, to a lesser degree, Uruguay are marked by antagonism between "the camp," or rural areas, and the cities of Buenos Aires and Montevideo. To these historical pressure groups a fourth has now been added—the labor unions, which have become highly important in recent decades in both Uruguay and Argentina.

The Argentine Army remained generally in the background during the latter years of the 19th

Century and the first three decades of the 20th. Since 1930, however, it has often been in the foreground. Here one must make plain what is meant by "the Army." Unlike Britain or the United States, Argentina has no standing army in the sense of regular enlisted men, except for certain specialist units and crack regiments. Of its peacetime force of 85,000 men, conscripts drafted for one year make up 65,000. These conscripts are liable to recall in an emergency until they reach the age of 45, and this provides a trained reserve of about 250,000 men.

THE regular Army consists of 5,000 career officers and 15,000 career N.C.O.s (noncommissioned officers), who provide the permanent framework of the country's six divisions. It is these 20,000 men who form "the Army" in the political sense, and although the officers of course exercise the greater influence, they need the cooperation of the N.C.O.s, who are in direct contact with the men. The role played by the N.C.O.s and the rank and file when the Army makes a political move was made plain in an encounter between a British resident of Buenos Aires and an Argentine soldier during the 1943 coup. As the British resident describes it: "I asked one unoccupied soldier, 'What's this revolution about? Fascist? Democratic? Pro-Ally? Pro-Axis?' He looked at me glumly. 'You ever been in the Army, *ché?* The other day the sergeant came into our barrack room and told us to get up, see, and put on full kit. Someone said, "What's up, sergeant?" The sergeant said, "You're marching to Buenos Aires, that's what." Well when the sergeant says I'm marching to Buenos Aires I march to Buenos Aires, I don't ask any . . . silly questions, eh?' "

The Argentine Army is well equipped—by World War II standards. In a nuclear age this means that its use against an external enemy is limited, and the conclusion is hard to avoid that its size can be attributed to its role in the nation's internal affairs. Nevertheless, for reasons which will be considered later, it is far less sure of itself than it was, and a repetition of the quick and virtually unopposed coups of 1930 and 1943 would now be impossible.

The Navy plays a lesser role in politics than the Army, but it, too, has its sense of "corporate identity" and its political attitude, rather different from the Army's. While the Army officers are mostly conservative in politics, Navy officers often profess a sort of humane liberalism. In internal affairs the Navy, when not keeping pointedly aloof and steaming haughtily out to sea "on maneuvers," has usually played a moderating or pacifying role.

The Argentine Air Force was formed as a separate entity only during the 1940s. Its young officers and N.C.O.s are much more interested in flying than in playing politics. A few years ago an R.A.F. flight sergeant, the pilot of the British air attaché's plane, who happened to eat in an Argentine Air Force mess, was invited by his messmates to drink to the toast, "Viva Churchill! Viva Perón!" "Are you all Peronistas?" he asked. "Of course not," was the reply. "But he got us the planes, no?" On most occasions when the Argentine Army has tried to get air support for an armed threat or a coup, the airmen have refused to become involved.

The armed forces of Uruguay for many years have played no political role. There is no conscription, and the three services are merely token forces. In an emergency the Army could muster a total strength, including reservists, of 120,000 men. The Navy has 450 officers and 1,500 enlisted men and has only nine vessels, all of them small. Uruguayans do not take their military service very seriously, nor do their neighbors. After the 1943 coup in Argentina a high Uruguayan official was asked what his Government would do if the Uruguayan forces tried anything of the same kind. "I should send a policeman to arrest them," he replied.

In Paraguay, on the other hand, the Army enjoys unparalleled prestige, both, ironically, for its heroic defeat in the 19th Century War of the Triple Alliance and for its equally heroic victory in the Chaco War of the 1930s. It has a panache quite lacking in the workaday Armies of the other two republics. It

also has the political say-so. The Paraguayan Army put General Stroessner into power in 1954, and in the last analysis it has been the Army that has kept him there. The President himself denies this, saying that he owes his power to the Colorado Party, which in turn owes its power to the will of the people. But this is the old dichotomy between theory and practice—although General Stroessner's claim that he enjoys the support of most of the people is not necessarily invalid.

The Paraguayan Army has 600 officers, 8,500 regular soldiers and 8,000 conscripts. The Navy, not surprisingly in a landlocked nation, is tiny: three armored river gunboats, two patrol boats and a few smaller vessels. Their principal task is the almost impossible one of preventing smuggling.

Of the role of the armed forces in the three republics, one could describe that of the Uruguayan as purely decorative and that of both the Argentine and the Paraguayan as traditional. Both of the latter have played the watchdog which is prepared to step in (generally in the conservative interest) to avoid chaos. And the Paraguayan Army did step in, frequently, throughout the 19th Century, and remains prepared to do so today. The Argentine Army has generally been more restrained, content for the most part to exercise its power behind the scenes. Until recently this role was accepted, and even approved, by a good portion of the Argentine public.

But the coup of 1930 and the later one of 1943 (which made possible Perón's rise to power) were a different matter. Both were military actions designed to overthrow constitutional civilian governments, and although the governments were not particularly popular with the general public, neither were the coups. The experience of military bungling after 1930 made some portions of the public actively hostile in 1943. The jokes about the 1943-1945 provisional

---

THE MILITARY ATTITUDE

"The crisis that afflicts many of our countries is a moral one rooted in lack of patriotism often poorly replaced by foggy concepts of nationalism. This makes it absolutely necessary for us to step in [and take over the government]."
—an Argentine admiral

"The basic mistake the U.S. makes in facing Latin America's current political problems is to believe that the alternative is between Communism and democracy. No. The alternative is between Communism and rightist dictatorship. There is no other solution."
—a Paraguayan colonel

"The entire world is in danger. Danger must be faced with facts, not words. We believe in action when politicians lose time in palavers. That is why we have to apply pressure from time to time and maintain it just as long as we deem necessary."
—an Argentine general

Government (which consisted largely of Army officers) were legion: the news broadcasts on the state radio were nicknamed "The Orders of the Day" and the story went around that the only generals who had not been given plum jobs were General Motors and General Electric.

This cynicism was increased by the fact that the military rulers could not seem to agree as to what was the purpose of their coup. Some of the members of the Army secret society called the GOU, which had engineered the 1943 coup, were patriotic but politically inexperienced men who simply felt that the previous Castillo Government had been inept to a disastrous degree. Many more feared that Castillo's successor would be a member of the old landed oligarchy. But the military regime was inept, too, and highhanded, and won the Army few friends. The Army continued to lose popular respect by its equivocal attitude throughout the Perón regime (the Navy remained consistently hostile). The Army's part in the eventual overthrow of Perón in 1955 earned it the enmity of organized labor. The Army-supported provisional presidencies of Generals Lonardi and Aramburu between 1955 and 1958 did something to refurbish the Army's tarnished image, but after the restoration of civilian rule and the election of Arturo Frondizi in 1958, the military's stock slumped again. The Army seemed incapable of leaving Frondizi alone and, divided within itself, pushed the civilian Government first this way and then that. Its clumsy ouster of Frondizi in 1962 made Argentines ashamed of the figure their country was cutting in the world.

From then until the election of Dr. Arturo Illia to the presidency in late 1963, the Army continued to lose face through internal squabbling over how to deal with the problem of the Peronistas. Since Illia's election, the continued threat of Army interference in what most citizens now consider purely civilian matters has further alienated public opinion.

IN many parts of Latin America the political influence of the military has been equaled by that of the Roman Catholic Church. In the River Plate, however, the Church has played a less important political role, although during the 19th Century it did make its influence felt, especially in the more conservative interior regions of Argentina. In recent times it was involved in both the rise and the fall of Perón.

There have been several reasons for this comparative lack of power. As the almost unheeded "Cinderella" of the Spanish Empire, whose worth was not apparent to the mother country, the River Plate was not the site of vast Church holdings as were the mineral-rich countries like Mexico and Peru. Also, whereas the Church in Peru and Mexico was faced with the immense task of dismantling the entire apparatus of established religions—the elaborate polytheistic cults of the Aztecs and the Inca—in the River Plate there was no such problem. The original inhabitants of the River Plate region were primitive peoples, without elaborate religious hierarchies, let alone powerful states to back them. Their beliefs were simple, and in any case their numbers were small and they lacked social organization. If politically recalcitrant, they could be eliminated by the civil power; if amenable, they were easy to convert. So the Church had no need to deploy its big battalions.

THIRDLY, there was not, as in Peru and Mexico, a proliferation of impressive pre-Christian temples. Therefore the Church did not need for prestige purposes to build equally impressive cathedrals and churches with a full complement of priests supplied with rich vestments and a complex liturgy. In addition, there was the region's sheer size. Out in the vast Pampa the Gauchos, who eventually formed the majority—or at any rate the trend-setting group—of the rural community, were unlikely to see a priest from one year's end to the other, and in so far as they did, they were likely to regard the priests as citified fellows with no understanding of the rural way of life.

A further, and most significant, reason for the Church's relative lack of power in the River Plate nations is the fact that for half of the 19th Century its ties with the Vatican were severed. This curious situation came about when many of the River Plate clergy, especially the Creoles, supported the region's drive for independence from Spain. A number of priests actively worked for the revolutionary cause and many of them contributed money to buy guns for San Martín's armies. The Holy See quite naturally sided with its old stronghold, ultraconservative Spain, and left the renegade Church in far-off South America to fend for itself.

But slowly the Church in the River Plate lost its revolutionary zeal and began more and more to lean to the side of the conservatives both in Buenos Aires and in the old provincial cities. This involvement of the Church with the conservative side led—as it did in many other parts of the world—to a measure of anticlericalism. This was especially common among 19th Century Italian immigrants to Argentina, many of whom had left their own country because of the obscurantism of current Vatican policy and its identification with reactionary Italian regimes. Some of their descendants to this day have inherited this opposition to the Church.

IN this century the Church became involved in politics notably during the era of Perón. It supported Perón's original candidacy in 1945, largely because it disapproved of the opposition parties, which included Communists as well as Radicals, Socialists and Progressive Democrats. The Church especially disliked those Radical and Socialist candidates who were said to advocate the separation of church and state, the abolition of religious education and the legalization of divorce.

Not very long after Perón had come to power, however, the Church's attitude began to change. The 1943 Government, of which Perón had been a member, had made religious instruction compulsory in state schools, and from the beginning of Perón's Administration priests were invited to give their blessing to party and labor-union meetings. But the Church began to be alarmed when the Government required state schoolteachers to tell their pupils that Peronismo was "the one true faith of all Argentines." Even worse was the virtual canonization of Eva Perón, whom schoolchildren were encouraged to call "Santa Evita."

Ironically, it was a comparatively enlightened measure of the Perón Government in September 1954 that initiated the final breach between the Roman Catholic Church and the state. This law gave illegitimate children the same rights as those born in wedlock—a reasonable provision in a country where divorce was (and is) unobtainable, and where

many ill-adjusted couples get divorced abroad, usually in Uruguay, and if they wish to marry someone else, do that in Uruguay as well. By a sort of gentleman's agreement, the newly married couples have rarely been prosecuted for adultery after returning, but under Argentina's strict inheritance laws the children of the second union were seriously penalized. Perón's new law rectifying this inequity seemed to many members of the priesthood to be an attack on the sanctity of family life and was thus declared unacceptable.

At the same time that this law was passed, Perón made a speech in which he accused the Church of interfering in labor relations and of trying to build up its own political party. Three months later, in December 1954, Perón legalized divorce. (This law has since been revoked.) The climax came in 1955 with the introduction of a bill which would have deprived the Church and all of its many educational establishments of their tax exemptions. In reply, religious demonstrators chanted "Christ or Perón." Perón retaliated by imprisoning priests and closing down Catholic newspapers. Because the Church is basically a middle-class institution, this gave a rallying point to the middle-class lawyers, university teachers, students, businessmen and Army officers who had their own reasons for disliking Perón, and it was this combination which succeeded in driving Perón from power.

IT was a pyrrhic victory for the Church, however, for the part it played in the overthrow of Perón lost it the support of the pro-Peronista majority of the working class. At the same time, its dilatoriness in denouncing Perón and its feebleness in opposing him diminished the respect in which the middle classes had held it. Argentina remains a Catholic country, and Roman Catholicism is still the nation's official established religion. The Church has special legal privileges and, unlike other denominations, does not pay taxes on its property. But in spite of its official position, the Argentine Church's political influence has become with the years more and more peripheral.

In Uruguay, as in Argentina, the impact of the Catholic Church has been historically far less than in many other parts of Latin America, and for many of the same reasons. Although Uruguay was and is about 90 per cent Roman Catholic, the Uruguayans have never been religious partisans, and their Church has seldom injected itself into the nation's politics. José Batlle y Ordóñez, the founder of modern Uruguay, had a skeptical attitude toward the Church. The Constitution of 1918, based on his ideas, officially separated church and state, removed any reference to the Deity from the presidential oath of office, and omitted the preamble to the earlier Constitution, which had invoked divine aid. It affirmed that the state supported no religion but allowed freedom of worship to all.

Even in small ways this secularization is evident. For instance, Holy Week is officially known in Uruguay as La Semana de Turismo, or Tourist Week. Naturally in such an atmosphere, there is no religious teaching, or even reference to religion, in state schools.

In Paraguay, on the other hand, Roman Catholicism is the official established religion. The Paraguayan Constitution, however, declares that all other religions are to be tolerated "if they are not contrary to public morality and order." There have been no large Church landholdings in Paraguay since the seizure of the Jesuit *reducciones* in the 18th Century.

THE power of the secular landholders in the River Plate has been largely confined to Argentina, where it was dealt a serious blow by the Perón Administration. But in earlier centuries, the big *estancieros*, or landholders, of the interior were a formidable force to be reckoned with. Almost as soon as the Spanish had been defeated and the River Plate region had become independent, the interior provinces insisted that they would not accept a strong central government in Buenos Aires (see Chapter 4), and more than once they declared their own independence from rule by the central Government. Again and again during the 19th Century, the metropolis of Buenos Aires and the people of the interior found themselves at loggerheads. For a time there were, in effect, two Argentinas, and even after the Constitution of 1853 was accepted by Buenos Aires, and the nation was unified, politicians from both the city and the provinces retained the power (and the

desire) to paralyze, or at least seriously delay, legislation the other group felt necessary. Thus many needed reforms were never passed or came too late.

The intransigence of the big landowners and other people of the provinces was fed by their pride in their Hispanic heritage and in their rugged individualism. They tended to look down on the immigrant-saturated coast and could not understand that, although agrarian societies such as their own could afford to remain unchanged, political and social change *must* accompany growing industrialization. The result of their intransigence was that the workers of the industrial cities—with no laws to protect them—were reduced to helpless poverty. Thus, as soon as a savior appeared, in the shape of Perón, the workers' long-pent-up resentments exploded and smashed—apparently forever—the landowners' political power.

THE influence of the *estancieros* has been largely replaced by that of powerful business interests on the one hand and that of the labor unions on the other. The latter are the major factor which any Argentine Government now has to take into account. Peronistas control many of the unions, and although they are divided between those who want "Peronismo without Perón" and those who would like Perón back, labor has become a powerful new pressure group and is likely to be the crucial factor in Argentine politics in the next few decades.

Uruguay, which also had (and still has) an *estanciero* class, albeit never so powerful a one as Argentina's, has also seen labor unions gain a considerable measure of influence in the country's politics. However, the Uruguayan labor unions have been a part of the national scene for so long, and the welfare state is so firmly established, that labor in Uruguay is less a pressure group than a recognized part of the public scene. It is to be hoped that before very long the unions in Argentina will, together with the Army, become a more constructive and less potentially obstructive force in the nation's politics. It is also to be hoped that after more than 150 years of independence, the days of rule by pressure groups may soon come to an end, so that the people may at last gain complete and unthreatened sovereignty.

Argentine soldiers guard Buenos Aires' Government Palace after the Army's General Aramburu was sworn in as President in 1955.

An Unfortunate History of Rule by the Military

One Argentine admiral has summed up the military's view of its role in national affairs by saying, ". . . we are trained from early youth to love our country, while politicians are trained to exploit it." It is this attitude which has caused River Plate military academies to be called "schools for presidents." Argentina suffers badly from the military malady. Five Army coups have unseated presidents since 1930, and every politician must tread softly, knowing that his

policies need military approval. Uruguay in the 19th Century suffered almost continuous rule by *caudillos*, or strongmen, but no military dictator has been in power since 1890. Paraguay has repeatedly been governed by generals since independence. While Paraguay's present dictator, General Stroessner, seems to favor eventual civilian participation in the Government, officers continue to receive special treatment, and the Army is able to make or break any regime.

125

ELECTED PRESIDENT, Arturo Frondizi *(center, with glasses)*, accompanied by dignitaries from other Latin American nations, reviews an Independence Day parade in Buenos Aires. Frondizi ran an able Government, but when he allowed Peronistas to run for office in Congressional and provincial elections, the Army deposed him to prevent the Peronistas from assuming office.

MILITARY GOVERNMENT CHIEF, General Pedro Aramburu works in the President's office as his Vice President, Admiral Isaac Rojas, looks on. Aramburu took over the Argentine presidency in 1955 shortly after Perón's downfall. In 1958 Aramburu allowed free elections, and Arturo Frondizi was swept into office with the help of the Peronistas, followers of Perón.

DETACHMENT OF TROOPS forms up in front of the Government Palace *(below)* during a 1962 scuffle between two Army factions for control of the Government. José Maria Guido, former president of the Argentine Senate, was handed the presidency after Frondizi was toppled. But military men fought each other for political supremacy during his puppet regime.

MODERATE LEADER, President Arturo Illia *(above)* talks to a coffee vendor who had interrupted a cornerstone-laying ceremony in Buenos Aires. Following his election in October 1963, Illia led Argentina on a moderate, quiet course. The military appeared to have devoted its attention solely to preventing a return to power by Peronistas—or by ex-dictator Perón himself.

A MARTIAL FLAVOR *permeates Paraguay's national affairs and the daily lives of its people*

SCHOOLGIRLS from a convent watch Independence Day ceremonies in Asunción *(above)*. In the background is one of the Paraguayan Navy's five gunboats, flag-bedecked for the occasion.

SCHOOLBOYS parade past a bandstand during the Independence Day celebrations *(left)*. Fifty per cent of Paraguay's budget is allotted to "national defense" and 27 per cent to education.

DICTATOR, General Alfredo Stroessner *(opposite, in uniform)* attends a ceremony with Brazilian officials at Asunción's airport. Brazil had given Paraguay's Air Force some training airplanes.

RESPLENDENT UNIFORMS remain a common sight on city streets, and give evidence in Paraguay and Argentina of Army influence

CHATTING IDLY, Argentine cavalrymen *(above),* in full-dress uniforms designed by the liberator San Martín, relax during a parade in Buenos Aires. Argentina's Army numbers 85,000, the Navy 21,500.

STANDING ALERTLY in jeeps, a group of high-ranking Paraguayan officers *(left)* awaits the arrival of General Stroessner for a parade. Officers are the most privileged and prosperous of all Paraguayan citizens.

SALUTING SMARTLY, men of the Uruguayan Air Force *(opposite)* take part in ceremonies celebrating the 40th anniversary of the Air Force's founding. The armed forces play a small role in Uruguayan life.

ART STUDENTS from the architecture school of the University of Buenos Aires sketch a harbor scene in La Boca, one of the city's waterfront districts. Populated largely by people of Italian descent, La Boca is Buenos Aires' Bohemian quarter.

9

Enthusiasm for the Arts

THE culture of the River Plate countries, in the widest sense of the word "culture," is the product of a curious amalgam of local and foreign influences. Traditional folk music and the dances it has inspired, including the famous tango, owe an obvious debt to the native soil that nurtured them. On the other hand, the region's literature, its painting and its "serious" music have been deeply influenced by European models, and only recently has the area developed its own distinctive, self-confident voice in these arts.

In fact, it can be said that the Rioplatenses have been less remarkable for their artistic output, whether inspired by native sources or derived from Europe,

than for their voracious but discriminating addiction to reading and for their appreciation of plays, novels, poems, paintings—especially those imported from overseas. Their cultural appetite is astonishing. The per capita consumption of books is extremely high; Buenos Aires is one of the three major Spanish-language publishing centers in the world (the others being Madrid and Mexico City); the theaters of Buenos Aires and Montevideo are both numerous and enthusiastically attended; and the Sunday supplements of the "quality" newspapers, which have very large circulations, are on a par with the most highbrow literary journals in the United States. These supplements also reflect the peoples' overwhelming interest in cultural events in Europe and North America, as well as in their native cities. Articles in the same issue of a Sunday *La Prensa* may cover a new novel from Britain, the theatrical season in Paris, an opera in New York, a film festival in Venice, architecture in Sweden and the works of a Spanish painter. But if on the whole the Rioplatenses are predominantly cultural consumers rather than producers, their creative achievements, especially in literature and popular music, are nonetheless considerable.

THE region's popular music and dance did not begin, as is sometimes assumed, with the tango, which was a late arrival on the scene. The first music, in fact, dates back to the preconquest Indians. But in Argentina only one of these Indian dances has survived, the *carnavalito*, which is danced by all social classes in the northwestern provinces. Other traditional Argentine dances, dating from after the arrival of the Spaniards, are the *chacarera*, once common to the whole country but now largely restricted to poor people in the north, and the *escondido*, a Gaucho dance once nationwide but now also seen mostly in the north.

The gradual withdrawal of these national dances to the poorest and most "hillbilly" part of the country is symptomatic. Improved communications have served to bring most Argentines into a cosmopolitan fold. As early as the 1940s, farm workers attending local dance halls sat out most of the Argentine dances—including the tango. In the last few years, however, there has been a remarkable revival of native dances, not in the country but in Buenos Aires. Hundreds of informal clubs for dancing have sprung up, and citified *porteños* have found themselves gyrating to the traditional rough guitar music of the interior. Known as *el boom folklórico*, this rediscovery of the nation's musical riches is part of a general revival of interest in everything to do with the Gaucho and with a simpler, more heroic past.

Uruguay, like Argentina, was early divided musically between the dominant city, in Uruguay's case Montevideo, and the interior. The Gauchos and other country people had their own native music and dance, while the people of Montevideo turned their ears and moved their feet to less rugged strains imported from Europe. According to the historian Russell Fitzgibbon: "European travelers visiting the capital as early as 1800 were agreeably surprised by the music rendered and the lovely voices heard at the *tertulias* or evening receptions in Montevideo." For dancing, the people of Montevideo favored the stately measures of the minuet.

The general decline of native music and dance in this century did not hold true for the famous tango, which has had a long and popular life. Its origin, fittingly enough, seems to be dual—both native and European. Combining elements borrowed from the Buenos Aires slums and from Spain, the tango first became popular at the beginning of the 20th Century. At that time it was urban and unrespectable, sung in the sleazy bars of La Boca, the dockside district of Buenos Aires where the Bohemians and the working class mixed, and where the tango was picked up by smart young men sowing their wild oats. Many of these young men subsequently went to Paris, where they introduced the tango to higher social circles. Thus given a social cachet, it returned to Argentina in about 1917 in its modern form and remained the most popular music in the region for more than 30 years, but it is now on the wane as Argentina turns to the pop tunes of Liverpool, London and New York or returns to earlier and more authentically native music.

EVEN in Paraguay popular music has been strongly affected by European trends and fashions. Indeed, most of the popular or folk dances are lighthearted versions of formal European steps transmuted by the Guarani temperament. As early as the middle of the 19th Century, people at the National Club in Asunción were dancing the waltz and the minuet. A lively form of the polka is perhaps Paraguay's most popular dance today. It is fortunate that Paraguayans do enjoy their polkas, for by a decree of President Stroessner in 1955, all orchestras were required to know, and play frequently, the "Colorado Polka," named after Stroessner's political party; the "26th of February Polka," which commemorates a Colorado coup of 1949; and, naturally, the "General Stroessner Polka."

Symphonic or "classical" music in the River Plate has been almost entirely imported. But the fact that the River Plate countries have themselves produced no Bachs or Beethovens does not mean that such music is not appreciated. The vast and stately Teatro Colón in Buenos Aires has long attracted opera singers from all over the world in the same way as do the Metropolitan in New York, London's Covent Garden and Milan's La Scala. In Uruguay the Government radio station not only broadcasts serious music but has established its own symphony orchestra and opera and ballet companies.

SIMILARLY, although the River Plate has not produced many writers of world stature, its citizens have always had a high appreciation of what has been produced elsewhere. Politicians, businessmen and even Army officers pay far more attention to literature and to culture in general than do their counterparts in the so-called Anglo-Saxon countries. Bartolomé Mitre, who was President of Argentina from 1862 to 1868, translated Dante, and the great writer and educational reformer Domingo Faustino Sarmiento was elected to Argentina's presidency in 1868 largely because of his cultural achievements. Perhaps most remarkable of all is Dr. Alfredo Palacios, who has been a flamboyant figure in the Argentine Socialist Party throughout the first half of the 20th Century; once president of the University of La Plata, he has written some 42 books and holds honorary professorships at half a dozen universities. Paraguayan politicians have a tradition of intellectualism and for generations have specialized in the writing of historical essays.

In addition to the intellectuals and the politicians, the ordinary people in Argentina and Uruguay have not only a remarkably high degree of literacy but also a considerably higher taste in what they read than is evident in most English-speaking countries. The bookstalls and newsstands in the subway stations in Buenos Aires, like those in London and New York, carry locally published paperbacks. But the ones in Buenos Aires do not have pictures of nearly nude women on their covers, and the popular authors include Shakespeare, Homer, Marcel Proust, Thomas Mann and Sinclair Lewis, besides local writers of high caliber.

This high level of literacy is reflected in the region's newspapers. For many years La Prensa of Buenos Aires has been ranked with The New York Times and The Times of London as one of the great dailies of the world. It is often dull, but it is essential reading for anyone who wants comprehensive news coverage; and its Sunday edition, as already mentioned, covers a wide cultural field. Besides La Prensa, Argentina has several other fine, enterprising newspapers, among them La Nación of Buenos Aires, La Capital of Rosario and La Nueva Provincia of Bahia Blanca. Uruguay, too, in spite of its small size and tiny population, has a remarkable number of serious and widely read newspapers. The best-known is El Día, founded in 1886 by Uruguay's great statesman José Batlle y Ordóñez.

River Plate literary production, as opposed to appreciation, is of comparatively recent growth. Apart from a few early chroniclers, such as Ruy Díaz de Guzmán (1554?-1629), there were almost no writers of consequence until after independence. The early postcolonial writers did not draw on native materials, but slavishly followed the literary fashions of Europe, particularly those of France. It was not until the late 19th Century that several Argentine writers opened Rioplatenses' eyes to the literary possibilities of their own homelands.

The most famous of these was José Hernández, author of the long epic poem Martín Fierro. Hernández extolled the free life of the roaming Gaucho on the boundless Pampa and reached a twofold public: the townsman who was far enough removed from the life of the land to be able to idealize it, and the countryman who was close enough to it to be able to identify with the hero of Hernández' epic. Hernández himself was no Gaucho, but a city dweller who had rebelled against the European domination of River Plate literature.

NOT all Hernández' contemporaries shared his views. The great educator Sarmiento, who was actually born in the interior, had only contempt for what he considered the barbarism of local culture and customs and tried to "civilize," i.e., Europeanize, his contemporaries. However, the mystique of Hernández' Gaucho world grew as its reality receded, and the mystique is still very much alive today. Curiously enough, the greatest gauchesco novel, Ricardo Güiraldes' Don Segundo Sombra, published in 1926, coincided with the very last days of the old Gaucho life on the Pampa. Although almost every Argentine can quote *Martín Fierro* and has read or heard of *Don Segundo Sombra,* the life depicted in these works is as remote from his own as the life of the old wild West is from the life of the average modern North American.

Güiraldes' great work marked not only the end of the Gaucho but also the beginning of a new era in River Plate literature. The 1920s and 1930s saw a reaction, not toward the European styles and themes of the early 19th Century writers, but to a new cosmopolitanism with a definite River Plate coloring. River Plate writers began to see themselves as *partners* in the European tradition rather than as mere admirers and imitators.

THE leading figure in this new movement was unquestionably the Argentine writer Jorge Luis Borges, who continues to be the greatest Spanish-language writer in South America and perhaps in the world. In his poems, essays and short stories, Borges shows his deep familiarity with European sources—his favorite philosophers are the Anglo-Irishman Berkeley, the Germans Kant and Schopenhauer, and the Italian Benedetto Croce—but he unmistakably is, and thinks of himself as, an Argentine author. He is not a "popular" writer in the sense that Hernández and Güiraldes were; the man in the street is unlikely ever to quote him. His style is meticulous, subtle and labyrinthine, and his themes are difficult ones: time, the nature of man, the meaning of the universe. But his influence on his fellow writers has been profound.

One of those influenced by Borges has been Eduardo Mallea, who, in his *Historia de una Pasión Argentina,* tried to define and elaborate just what the national experience adds up to—what it means to be an Argentine. Others have included a large group of lyric poets. In fact, until the recent appearance of several excellent fiction writers, including Ernesto Sábato, Julio Cortázar and W. G. Wéyland, lyric poetry has been the genre in which, by and large, River Plate writers have done their best work. Many of the pioneering efforts of these writers have been published by Victoria Ocampo, who founded and still edits the cultural magazine *Sur (South).* She is one of the most cosmopolitan of Argentine literary figures, as much at home in Britain as in Buenos Aires and as fluent in French as in Castilian.

Uruguay is, if possible, even more convinced of its lofty cultural, and especially literary, achievements than Argentina. But the truth is that throughout the 19th Century, Uruguayan intellectuals, like the Argentines, followed closely the patterns set by contemporary Europe. One of the half dozen writers who did deal directly and simply with Uruguayan life was José Alonso y Trelles (1857-1924), who, as his pen name, *"El Viejo Pancho"* (Old Pancho), suggests, wrote regional poetry dealing with the Gauchos in Gaucho vocabulary.

But the man who most influenced Uruguayan literature was José Enrique Rodó (1872-1917). Like Borges in Argentina, Rodó was a difficult writer, but his style had a deceptive appearance of simplicity, which laid his work open to misinterpretation. For instance, his philosophical essay *Ariel,* published in 1900, dealt with the interrelation of reason and spirit, represented by Caliban and Ariel, characters in Shakespeare's *Tempest.* But coming just after the Spanish-American War of 1898, it was seen as an allegory of the struggle between the rich but materialist United States and poor but spiritual Latin America.

THE most considerable Uruguayan poet is usually acknowledged to be Juan Zorrilla de San Martín, who died in 1931. Basically a romantic, Zorrilla is difficult to classify, and critics have argued whether his major work, *Tabaré,* is an epic poem, a verse novel or something else. Its hero is the mestizo son of a Charrua Indian chief and a Spanish woman, and the action takes place during the period when the Indians were a fast-vanishing race in Uruguay. Like Rodó's *Ariel,* it is symbolic; the Charrua represent natural creation, the Spaniards the human spirit; the latter triumphs. Uruguay has also had two quite remarkable women poets. One, Delmira Agustini, celebrated the physical delights of love in the most outspoken terms in almost all her poems, but her imagery is so brilliant that the poems transcend and spiritualize their subject matter. Juana de Ibarbourou, also a fine poet, wrote of the seasons and of youth, maturity, old age and decay.

In Paraguay, as elsewhere, Spanish-language literature in colonial times tended to follow European models, and little work of value was produced. Some Guarani-language writing has been highly praised by those who speak Guarani, which has been called "one of the most expressive and elegant [languages] in the world." So it may be, but outside Paraguay only people in the Argentine Province of Corrientes and parts of neighboring Bolivia can understand it.

Later Spanish-language literature in Paraguay has tended to lag behind Argentina and Uruguay in its content and philosophy. Since the end of the brutal Chaco War in 1935, however, Paraguayan literature has shown a new and remarkable vigor. Following the lead of Herib Campos Cervera and Josefina Pla, a dedicated group of poets has grown up. And beginning in 1951 with Gabriel Casaccia's *La babosa (The Foolish Woman)*, a body of quite superior fiction has been produced. The best-known and most respected of these new writers is Augusto Roa Bastos, whose *Hijo de hombre (Son of Man)* has been called "the most important book that has appeared in Paraguay in recent times."

This widespread creative activity, as well as the unusually high level of cultural awareness that characterizes the River Plate nations, reflects a high average standard of education, far higher than in most of the rest of Latin America. In Argentina, thanks largely to Sarmiento, primary education up to the age of 14 is universal, and the same is true of urban Uruguay. Paraguay until recently lagged far behind, but since 1957 a new drive of school building and modernization of teaching methods has been under way. Secondary education has now become widespread throughout the River Plate, and university enrollment is high. In Argentina, there are universities in Buenos Aires, La Plata, Córdoba and Mendoza, and in most of the other large provincial cities. There are also a number of technical and agricultural

schools. Uruguay has only one university, in Montevideo, but it is one of the largest in Latin America. Paraguay has a distinguished university in Asunción.

The River Plate universities have traditionally concentrated on literature, law and medicine and have neglected painting and the plastic arts. Perhaps partly for this reason, there was until recently little painting or sculpture of value done in the River Plate countries. However, this has changed radically in the last few years. Argentina now has a large group of talented young Expressionist painters, and Buenos Aires has suddenly become to South American artists what Paris was to artists from all over the world in the era before World War I. Argentine painters exhibit their works in New York and Paris and win medals at international culture festivals.

River Plate sculpture suffered for more than a century from the fact that most of it was commissioned by presidents and public authorities with traditional tastes, who liked to put heroes on horses in public places. However, tastes are changing, and while Uruguay remains fond of the works of José Belloni, long the country's leading sculptor, they are also proud of a group of younger and more experimental artists. Argentina has several sculptors whose works have drawn praise in European exhibitions and have been bought by museums both at home and abroad.

The theater in the River Plate, like painting, has seen a startling upsurge in activity in recent decades. The center of this theatrical activity is, of course, Buenos Aires, which has no fewer than 20 full-fledged theaters, compared to about 30 in present-day New York, as well as about 30 lesser houses similar to New York's "off Broadway" establishments. The *porteños* have a voracious appetite for plays, especially the latest and most avant-garde pieces from Europe and the United States. All of the plays of the Romanian author Eugene Ionesco have been

AN ECCENTRIC BRITISH GAUCHO

One of the most noted writers, and most eccentric characters, in Argentine literary history was not an Argentine at all, but the adventurous son of a Scottish laird named Robert Bontine Cunninghame Graham. Born in 1852, Cunninghame Graham went to Argentina at the age of 17, where he rode with the Gauchos and became a smuggler of horses. His dashing feats and aristocratic good looks prompted Argentine newsmen to call him the "Don Quixote of the Pampa." He subsequently moved on to Mexico City, where (under the alias of "Professor Bontini") he taught fencing, and to Texas, where he was a cowpoke. Returning to Britain, he became a Member of Parliament and an important organizer of the Independent Scottish Labour Party. His literary works include many sketches of Pampa life and a valuable and entertaining history, *The Conquest of the River Plate*. He died in 1936 in Argentina.

produced in Buenos Aires, as have all the savage satires of the Swiss Friedrich Düerrenmatt, the weird and bitter comedies of Irishman Samuel Beckett and the angry plays of England's foremost angry young man, John Osborne. There have been many productions of plays by such U.S. authors as Arthur Miller, Tennessee Williams, Truman Capote and Thornton Wilder. Works by a large number of Argentine playwrights—some of whom are also actors—have been produced: in all, some 58 different Argentine plays were brought to the stage during the 1963 season.

THE most remarkable segment of the Argentine theater is the cooperatives—small acting companies which share expenses and profits, if any, among themselves and perform in basements, empty churches, or even outdoors in courtyards or in the street, beneath Spanish-style balconies. Here young writers have a chance to have their plays produced and young actors to gain experience.

The Argentine Government helps spur this activity through a fund for the arts, which is financed largely by a special 5 per cent tax on all advertising presented on either radio or television. In 1963 the fund doled out $200,000 to further the drama, giving scholarships for study abroad to promising playwrights, bringing budding actors in from the provinces to work in the Buenos Aires theater and sending city-trained actors out to provincial theater companies.

In short, Buenos Aires shares with the provinces a theater which for both quality and quantity rivals that of New York, Paris or London. Some of this creative energy has spilled over into the Argentine film industry, which is second only to Mexico's in the output of Spanish-language films. After a slow start in the 1930s, when tango-spangled melodramas were their standard product, Argentine film makers have become not only prolific but highly sophisticated. Hugo del Carril has become a director of considerable power, and the works of Leopoldo Torre Nilsson are acclaimed at film festivals all over the world. Unfortunately Torre Nilsson's bitter and implacable studies of Argentine society are not widely distributed, and they are seldom shown in New York or London, let alone Minneapolis or Liverpool.

This insularity on the part of overseas countries is not reciprocated in the River Plate, where the films

showing at the major first-run houses in a typical week may come from half a dozen different countries. It is interesting that when dubbing Spanish dialogue into Hollywood films was tried in the major River Plate cities in the 1940s, it was a complete failure. First-run houses advertising films *"totalmente hablada en español"* were half empty, and scruffy neighborhood theaters cashed in by proclaiming that their shows were *"totalmente hablada en inglés"* (completely spoken in English). The people of Buenos Aires and Montevideo huffily pointed out that they could read subtitles, if necessary, and that they did not want to hear Spencer Tracy acting the part of a German in Spanish with a Mexican accent.

Rioplatenses do not, of course, spend all of their spare time listening to music, reading, attending the theater, going to the movies or dancing the newly revived folk dances. And for a good reason: they are crazy about sports. And of all the sports, *fútbol* (sometimes pronounced *foba*) is king.

The name, of course, was originally spelled football, but the sport has nothing to do with the game of that name played in the United States. It is association football, or soccer, introduced from Britain in the 19th Century and adopted, accepted and adapted by the River Plate countries.

IT is hard for an outsider to believe the enthusiasm, indeed the mania, of the River Plate soccer fans, who on any given Sunday will crowd to overflowing not one but a dozen stadiums. The players show a corresponding flair and can more than hold their own in competition with the best teams from Britain, France or Italy. In fact, an all-star team from Uruguay—Montevideo is quite as soccer-mad as Buenos Aires—has won four international football cups.

The sports enthusiasts of the River Plate do not confine themselves to soccer, but also love horse racing (and betting), Rugby, tennis and a variety of water sports. And the Argentines have a hair-raising game called *Pato*, which combines elements of polo—it is played on horseback—and basketball. If there is any truth in the stereotype of the "passionate Latin temperament," the image will be represented in the realm of sports, where the usually controlled and cosmopolitan people of the River Plate most clearly show their true selves.

MASTERFUL STYLIST, Jorge Luis Borges writes subtle, intricate short stories, poems, novels and philosophical essays. Now totally blind, he dictates to a secretary.

Growing Vigor in the World of the Arts

For many decades the artists in the River Plate slavishly emulated European styles and themes. But then with the discovery of the Gaucho and other native subject matter, the arts in Argentina and Uruguay began finally to come of age. With at least 200 painters of note, Buenos Aires has become a center of Latin American art. Argentina boasts a renowned composer in Alberto Ginastera, a fine film director in Leopoldo Torre Nilsson and possibly the leading Spanish-language writer in Jorge Luis Borges. River Plate culture is at last finding its true voice.

MAJOR NOVELIST, Argentina's Ernesto Sábato leaped to prominence with his first book, *The Tunnel*, published in 1948 and since translated into six languages.

PIONEERING EDITOR, Victoria Ocampo *(right),* the *grande dame* of Argentine letters, publishes the influential literary magazine *Sur,* which she founded in 1931.

GIFTED ARTISTS *find enthusiastic audiences for their work in cosmopolitan Buenos Aires*

A PROBING FILM MAKER, Leopoldo Torre Nilsson *(above)* stands on the terrace of his apartment with his wife. His film *Hand in the Trap* won the 1961 Cannes Film Critics Award.

AN EXPERIMENTAL COMPOSER of international fame, Alberto Ginastera *(left)* teaches a music class at Buenos Aires' Center for Higher Musical Studies, which he founded in 1961.

A GLITTERING AUDIENCE waits for the curtain to go up at the gilt-and-plush Teatro Colón *(opposite)* in Buenos Aires, one of the world's largest and most illustrious opera houses.

*A NEW GENERATION of
inventive painters is making
the River Plate area
a force in the plastic arts*

DELICATE COLORS illuminate an agitated painting *(above)* entitled *Charge* by Sarah Grilo of Buenos Aires. Miss Grilo used to paint in a strictly abstract style, but she recently began employing letters and numbers as motifs.

JAGGED SHAPES vibrate in an abstraction *(left)* by Kazuya Sakai, an Argentine of Japanese parentage. Sakai, who has worked in New York since 1963, won a gold medal for painting at the 1958 Brussels World's Fair.

VERSATILE CRAFTSMAN, Carlos Páez Vilaró (right) displays one of his paintings at his vacation house near Punta del Este, Uruguay. Besides painting, Vilaró sculpts, works in ceramics, composes music, and writes both poetry and prose. He is curator of Montevideo's distinguished Museum of Modern Art, which he founded.

BOLD INNOVATOR, Rómulo Macció peers over one of his paintings in the garden of his Buenos Aires home. His canvases often feature skull-like heads, and his slashing brushwork is characteristic of the works of other members of Macció's "school," the Neo-Figurativists. Macció has had seven one-man shows in Buenos Aires.

143

ROUGH PATAGONIAN LANDSCAPE is part of a ranch that grazes 46,000 sheep, some of which are here driven into a corral by a herdsman and his dogs. Even the windbreaks of poplars scarcely temper the impact of the immense, bare landscape.

10
Turning toward New Loyalties

ALTHOUGH the River Plate countries belong to all the major regional bodies such as the Organization of American States, they have traditionally been more orientated toward Europe than toward any American country, north or south. This aloof attitude toward their neighbors is reflected in a tendency among Rioplatenses in general and Argentines in particular to be vague about continental geography beyond their own borders. Less-educated Argentines may refer to Ecuador, Colombia and Venezuela as "Central American" countries, and are not particularly interested if corrected. *"Es lo mismo,"* they say—"It's all the same." About Europe, particularly among Argentines and Uruguayans, there is no

such ignorance. Most Rioplatenses have fairly accurate stereotypes of Britons, Germans, Poles, Frenchmen and Scandinavians. They can point out most European countries on a map and name the capitals of half a dozen of them. More than this, when it comes to Spain and Italy they will distinguish between the various regions and their inhabitants: the Basques, they will tell you, are industrious, the people of Madrid proud and the Milanese pushy.

The Spanish spoken in the River Plate, too, despite its "Gaucho" modifications of purely local origin, has absorbed far more European (and far fewer North American) words and phrases than has the speech of most other Latin American nations. *"Piano*

piano'' (Take it easy), *''Se non te vedo più felice morte''* (If I don't see you again, happy death) and similar Italianisms are common. British influence on terminology is strong, notably in connection with railroads. Crossties are not *traviesas* but *durmientes,* apparently from the English word ''sleeper.'' The same is true of sports terminology—and the sports of the River Plate derive principally from England and owe almost nothing to the United States or even Spain. Finally, and symptomatically, while most other Latin American countries use American English in correspondence and bilingual publications, the River Plate countries use the style and spelling favored in Britain.

ALL this applies chiefly to Argentina and Uruguay, since Paraguay has been largely isolated from outside influences. There are historical reasons why these two republics should look back across the Atlantic rather than to the north toward their sister Latin countries and the United States. The early Spanish settlers depended in almost every sense on the Old World. In the 19th Century the development of communications and public services by British and to some extent French and Belgian interests increased the transatlantic ties, as did the massive wave of immigration from Western Europe.

Politically speaking, although the North American Revolution was one of the events that inspired the River Plate's assertion of independence, the philosophy behind the move was that of the French revolutionaries. The new nations, furthermore, grew up during a period when France was the dominant cultural influence in the Western world, and Argentina and Uruguay imported everything from textbooks to ladies' dresses from Paris. During the same period, Britannia ruled the waves, so that the Argentine naval tradition laid down by its founder, Admiral Brown, continued to be a largely British one. At the turn of this century, when the Armies of all three republics became effectively organized, Germany had become the world's leading military power, so that it was natural that the River Plate nations should seek German advice and assistance in the training and organization of their land forces. This Germanic influence is still evident today in the Armies of both Argentina and Paraguay.

This habit of copying or adapting European models became established in a period when the United States was not yet a predominant power in the Americas, let alone in the world as a whole. The Monroe Doctrine, although an important declaration of U.S. policy, was not backed up by a strong naval force, and the River Plate countries continued to rely on the large British Navy to protect them against any possible Spanish attempt at a *reconquista.*

FOR all these reasons the Rioplatenses were and are predisposed to think in European terms. World War I, which had pursued its murderous course for three years before the United States's entry, did nothing to change this attitude. Though none of the three countries went to war on the Allied side, Argentina and Uruguay were Britain's major suppliers of meat, and several thousand Anglo-Argentines and Anglo-Uruguayans joined the British forces. Very few German-Argentines went to fight for the fatherland, and Argentine public opinion tended to be hostile to the families of those who did.

The pattern in World War II was very much the same, although this time a highly vocal segment of the Argentine public sympathized with Germany. These people could generally be described as conservative nationalists, and they saw in fascism, especially of the type imposed on Spain by Franco, certain elements that they would have liked to see in Argentina, such as rule by a coalition of the Army and the Church. This idea appealed, naturally, to both the Argentine officer corps and the clergy, who, by and large, were at least mildly pro-Axis. The military-dominated governments of the era were of the same mind. All of these groups were skillfully played upon by German propaganda. But the majority of the Argentine people were pro-Allied and impatient with the governments' attitude, especially where this seemed to put Argentina in a less than dignified position.

Argentine public feeling, indeed, was much more strongly pro-Allied during World War II than it had been in World War I, and the Government was forced to countenance activities by Allied sympathizers which went far beyond the normal latitude of neutrality. The Anglo-Argentines, for example, set up a British Community Council which levied its own tax from Anglo-Argentines and British residents and used the proceeds to further the war effort. Throughout the war various groups sympathetic to the Allied cause staged an ambitious annual *Feria de Buena Voluntad,* or Goodwill Fair, which was attended by thousands of ordinary Argentine citizens.

One reason, of course, for this far greater Argentine emotional involvement in World War II was a basic revulsion against Nazi totalitarianism, coupled with the shock caused by the fall of France, long Argentina's "spiritual mother." In Uruguay, whose wartime governments were consistently pro-Allied, public sentiment was even more anti-Axis than in Argentina, while official action, though keeping to the letter of neutrality, constantly interpreted it in the Allied interest.

A FINE example of Uruguay's interpretation of its neutral role in such a way as to benefit the Allies occurred after the famous naval battle of the River Plate in 1939. In this battle, which took place off Punta del Este, two British cruisers, *Ajax* and *Exeter,* and a New Zealand ship, the *Achilles,* damaged the German pocket battleship *Graf Spee.* The *Graf Spee* limped into Montevideo harbor, and her captain demanded that he be allowed to remain long enough not only to make his vessel seaworthy, but also to repair his guns and control systems so that he would have a chance in a renewed battle with the British ships waiting for him outside the Plate estuary.

The Uruguayan Government did allow the Germans a short extension above the 24-hour limit normal in cases in which a belligerent vessel seeks refuge in a neutral harbor. But, despite considerable diplomatic pressure, the Uruguayans absolutely refused to give the Germans enough time to repair the *Graf Spee*'s armaments properly. Even when rumors circulated that the Germans had threatened to shell Montevideo, the Government remained adamant and the people, with blithe unconcern, went about their business. As a result, the Germans sailed when told to and, rather than tackle the British with their battered ship, scuttled the *Graf Spee* in the approaches to Montevideo harbor.

It is clear from this summary that the Rioplatenses, because of their European backgrounds, saw World War II largely as a repetition of the first, in which the Western European theater was all-important. The Soviet Union—a shadowy giant—seemed particularly remote, although the newspapers and radio stations gave due space and time to the Russian front. The Japanese attack on Pearl Harbor did arouse public outrage and a sudden outflow of sympathy for the United States, yet it was difficult for Rioplatenses to reconcile their peacetime image of the United States, built up from films and advertisements and shiny magazines, with the reality of a nation at war. The British tommy and the French poilu were familiar concepts; the G.I. was not.

United States propaganda did its best to sell South Americans the idea that they had a continental involvement in the war, with slogans like *"Las Américas unidas, unidas vencerán"* (The Americas united, united will win), but the River Plate nations were not yet ready to take an active part in the conflict. As the war drew to a close, however, Paraguay, Uruguay and to some extent Argentina began more and more to feel involved *as American nations.* The immediate cause was the requirement, laid down at Yalta in 1945, that they declare war on the Axis in order to qualify for admission to the United Nations conference at San Francisco. The United States was eager for all the Latin American countries to join the U.N. in order to have a solid Western bloc to match the expected Soviet-centered one. The River Plate nations complied, but with varying degrees of reluctance. On the day that Argentina declared war, March 27, 1945, a high Government official is reputed to have said as he left a meeting, "Today we are in mourning; we have to declare war."

THE principal cause for this reluctance in Argentina was, of course, the Government's vague but nonetheless real sympathy for the Axis cause. Paraguay and Uruguay were less hesitant; they had severed relations with the Axis powers some time before and now beat Argentina by also declaring war sooner. But there was a feeling among the people of all three countries that it was a needless and rather undignified gesture, tantamount to kicking a man when he is down, and none of them liked the idea of having their diplomatic moves dictated by other nations. But all three were anxious to play a part in the founding of a United Nations organization in which the smaller nations would have an effective voice, and their votes would be worth as much as anybody else's.

The global nature of the war eventually drove home to the Rioplatenses the fact that they were inextricably linked to the fate not only of the Americas but of mankind. The dropping of the atom bombs on Hiroshima and Nagasaki sealed the issue: no nation in such an age could afford to turn its back on the rest of the world.

THE River Plate countries thus emerged from the war with a far wider horizon than they had had before it, and this horizon now included the United States. There was, however, a different emphasis as far as international policy was concerned. The United States seemed to the Rioplatenses to be overly concerned with the "Red menace." The Rioplatenses did not see Russia as a threat, largely because they did not consider their own countries in danger of internal Communist subversion (as many Chileans, for instance, *did*). They had some reason for this equanimity. In Argentina the frustrations and resentments that might have fostered Communism had been channeled off by Peronismo, and the Argentine Communist Party was a negligible political factor—although it has since become larger. Even had it been more important than it was, it had a strong "national" tendency long before Tito or Togliatti advocated separate roads to socialism and would thus have been unlikely to toe the Moscow line.

Uruguay at the time was even less worried, believing its middle-class, welfare-state democracy sufficient insulation against any Communist lures. It has recently become less complacent, being the target of a barrage of Soviet propaganda. Paraguay, comparatively poor and backward, might have been expected to be more open to Communist penetration, but here again there were mitigating factors. Paraguay has neither a large urban proletariat nor a large group of landless peasants. And Paraguayan national feeling is in any case unfavorable to Communism, whatever its merits or demerits as a system, because it is an alien creed. If Karl Marx had been a Paraguayan, things might have been different. In addition, President Stroessner prides himself on being the toughest anti-Communist in the hemisphere, jailing

any Reds he discovers, so as "to promote social hygiene." The triumph of Fidel Castro's revolution in Cuba in January 1959 was, however, initially welcomed in the River Plate, particularly among intellectuals and students. This was because the revolution was at first seen as the triumph of David over Goliath, of the people over a brutal dictatorship, and also as an affirmation of Latin American national sovereignty, since it was known that Batista until nearly the end had enjoyed U.S. support or at any rate toleration.

But doubts began to set in as Castro moved nearer and nearer to the Soviet bloc, and enthusiastic young Rioplatenses who had gone to help build the new Cuba began to drift, disillusioned, homeward. The disenchantment was completed, outside all but the most far-left circles, by the Cuban crisis of 1962, when it became evident that Castro, far from being a possible continental leader of Latin American progress, was not even a free agent.

Since then there have been sporadic attempts by small groups of pro-Fidelistas to stir up trouble in the River Plate. This does worry the three Governments to some extent since, while Russia is distant and Marxism an alien ideology, Castro and his revolution are Latin American and his "reforms" seem to some River Plate workers to be relevant to their situation.

THE River Plate countries consider themselves part of a Western Christian tradition, and at the same time they value highly their own individual independence and sovereignty. For many years they have had a tendency to feel themselves separate from, and rather superior to, all the other American nations. This tendency toward self-isolation has shown signs in the last few years, however, of breaking down. All three nations, but especially Argentina and Uruguay, have a great deal to offer Latin America, from oil and automobiles to poets and advanced political ideas. They could become examples of progress to the whole continent, in the same way that Mexico is an example to Central America. At the moment, perhaps, Argentina is too unsure of itself, Uruguay too plagued by a stuttering economy and Paraguay too undeveloped to play this sort of a leading role. But the potentiality for leadership is there and hopefully will soon manifest itself.

Elegant operagoers congregate in the lounge for coffee, cigarettes and gossip during an intermission at Buenos Aires' Teatro Colón.

THE HIGH CIVILIZATION attained by many people of the larger cities . . .

The 200-foot-high Iguazú Falls pour over a ridge more than two miles long in the jungle near the Argentine-Paraguayan border.

A hydrofoil (opposite), skimming passengers across the River Plate from Colonia, Uruguay, approaches smog-shrouded Buenos Aires.

. . . remains remote from both the rural and urban poor, but the countries' vast natural

riches and increasing technological skills promise a greater measure of good for all

151

Appendix

HISTORICAL DATES

1493-1494 Papal bulls divide the New World between Spain and Portugal, giving Spain rights to the River Plate region. The line of demarcation is clarified in 1494 by the Treaty of Tordesillas between Spain and Portugal

1516 Juan Díaz de Solís, the first European to set foot in the River Plate area, lands on the coast of Uruguay and is killed by Indians

1520 Magellan, on his way around the world, sails into the mouth of the River Plate and renames it Río de Solís

1526-1530 Sebastian Cabot, in the service of Spain, explores the rivers emptying into the Plate estuary. He gives the River Plate its final name

1536 A small, short-lived settlement is founded by Pedro de Mendoza on the site of present-day Buenos Aires

1536-1596 Spanish settlers, many crossing the Andes from Peru, establish settlements in Argentine and Paraguayan territory. The settlements remain politically and economically dependent on distant Lima

1537 Members of an expedition from Buenos Aires found Asunción, which becomes for a time the most important settlement in the River Plate area

1580 An expedition from Asunción, led by Juan de Garay, refounds the port city of Buenos Aires

1588 The first Jesuit missionaries arrive in Asunción and proceed into the wilderness, where they soon set up *reducciones*—missions designed to bring the Indians into the Roman Catholic fold

1620 All settlements south of the confluence of the Paraguay and Paraná Rivers are gathered into the separate district of Río de la Plata, ruled by the viceroy of Peru, but with a governor in Buenos Aires

1726 Montevideo is founded by the governor of Buenos Aires as a bastion against the Portuguese to the north in Brazil

1767 Jesuits are banned from Spanish territory by King Charles III. The *reducciones* are gradually broken up

1776 Separate Viceroyalty of the Río de la Plata is created by Spain

1806-1807 British troops occupy Buenos Aires but are quickly defeated. A second invasion attempt is equally unsuccessful. The British occupy Montevideo for seven months but finally agree to leave

1810 The wars of independence begin on May 25, when the people of Buenos Aires create a separate government and reject the rule of the Spanish viceroy

1811 Paraguay declares itself independent of Spain

1811-1814 José Gervasio Artigas, assuming command of Uruguay's army, also breaks with the Buenos Aires Government

1814-1820 Troops from Buenos Aires defeat the forces of the Spanish viceroy in Montevideo. In 1815 Artigas' army drives the Argentines from Montevideo, but his forces are eventually beaten by Portuguese troops from Brazil

1816-1819 A congress meets in Tucumán and declares Argentina's independence from Spain. The congress writes Argentina's first Constitution

1817-1821 General José de San Martín, commander of the Argentine army, daringly crosses the Andes and defeats the Spanish in two major battles. Having freed Chile, he proceeds to attack Peru and takes the viceregal capital of Lima

1820-1828 Brazil annexes Uruguay. In 1825 Uruguayan refugees from Buenos Aires, reinforced by Argentine troops, cross the River Plate and precipitate a land-and-sea war between Argentina and now-independent Brazil. Finally, under pressure from Great Britain, the warring nations make peace and establish an independent Uruguay

1826-1869 Argentina adopts a system of laws governing the holding of land which allows influential men to gain control of huge ranches, amass fortunes and form a powerful oligarchy

1829-1852 Argentina is ruled by the dictator Juan Manuel de Rosas except for the years 1832 to 1835

1852 Rosas is toppled and sent into exile. An Argentine Constitution is drawn up in 1853, modeled on that of the United States

1857 The first railroad in Argentina begins operations

1865-1870 Argentina joins with Brazil and Uruguay to virtually destroy Paraguay, which had provoked the War of the Triple Alliance

1889-1892 The Civic Union of Youth and later the Radicals, both liberal political parties, challenge for the first time the rule of the oligarchy in Argentina

1903 José Batlle y Ordóñez starts the first of two terms as President of Uruguay during which he fashions the welfare state and ushers in a new era of stability

1912 The Saenz Peña Law in Argentina institutes universal male suffrage. The newly enfranchised voters help the Radicals, under Hipólito Irigoyen, to come to power in 1916

1914-1918 World War I: Argentina and Paraguay remain neutral. Uruguay breaks relations with Germany in 1917

1916-1930 The Radicals rule Argentina. Irigoyen is twice elected to the presidency. His corrupt and inefficient regime is overthrown by the military in 1930

1932-1935 Paraguay defeats Bolivia in the brutal Chaco War

1939-1945 Era of World War II: Paraguay and Uruguay remain neutral until they break relations with the Axis in 1942; all three River Plate nations declare war on the Axis in 1945

1943-1945 Military regimes rule Argentina for two years

1945 Juan Perón is swept to power in Argentina by the votes of the nation's workers. The Perón Government is dictatorial but passes many laws beneficial to the long-neglected laboring class

1951 The office of president is abolished in Uruguay and is replaced by an executive council

1952 Perón's wife and invaluable ally, Evita Perón, dies of cancer; resistance to Perón's dictatorship begins to stiffen

1954 General Stroessner becomes President of Paraguay

1955 Military revolt overthrows Perón

1955-1958 Two Army-led regimes rule in Argentina

1958-1962 Arturo Frondizi is President of Argentina until his overthrow by the Army

1963 Arturo Illia is elected Argentine President

FOR FURTHER READING

CHAPTER 1: THE THREE REPUBLICS

Bailey, Helen Miller, and Abraham P. Nasatir, *Latin America; the Development of Its Civilization*. Prentice-Hall, 1960.

Bridges, E. Lucas, *Uttermost Part of the Earth*. Hodder & Stoughton, London, 1948.

Davies, Howell, ed., *The South American Handbook, 1964*. Rand McNally, 1964.

Graham, R. B. Cunninghame, *Rodeo*. The Literary Guild, 1936.

Herring, Hubert, *A History of Latin America*. Alfred A. Knopf, 1962.

Hudson, W. H., *Far Away and Long Ago*. E. P. Dutton, 1942.

James, Preston E., *Latin America*. The Odyssey Press, 1959.

Rippy, J. Fred, *Latin America; A Modern History*. University of Michigan Press, 1958.

Schurz, William Lytle, *Latin America; A Descriptive Survey*. E. P. Dutton, 1963.

CHAPTER 2: NATIVES AND IMMIGRANTS

Graham, R. B. Cunninghame, *The Conquest of the River Plate*. Doubleday, Page, 1924.

Levene, Ricardo, *A History of Argentina*. University of North Carolina Press, 1937.

Mulhall, E. T. and M. G., *Handbook of the River Plate Republics*. Edward Stanford, London, 1875.

Nichols, Madaline W., *The Gaucho*. Duke University Press, 1942.

Raine, Philip, *Paraguay*. Scarecrow Press, 1956.

Rennie, Ysabel F., *The Argentine Republic*. Macmillan, 1945.

Sarmiento, Domingo F., *Life in the Argentine Republic in the Days of the Tyrants*. Hafner, 1960.

Scobie, James R., *Argentina; A City and a Nation*. Oxford University Press, 1964.

Sherbinin, Betty de, *The River Plate Republics*. Coward-McCann, 1947.

Steward, Julian H., ed., *Handbook of South American Indians*. United States Government Printing Office, 7 vols., 1946-1959.

CHAPTERS 3 AND 4: HISTORY

Bannon, John Francis, and Peter Masten Dunne, *Latin America; an Historical Survey*. Bruce Publishing Company, 1947.

Chaves, Julio César, *Compendio de Historia Paraguaya*. Edición del Autor, Buenos Aires, 1960. *(Only in Spanish.)*

Ferns, H. S., *Britain and Argentina in the Nineteenth Century*. Oxford University Press, 1960.

Fitzgibbon, Russell H., *Uruguay*. Rutgers University Press, 1954.

Haring, C. H., *The Spanish Empire in America*. Oxford University Press, 1947.

Kirkpatrick, F. A., *A History of the Argentine Republic*. Cambridge University Press, 1931.

Levene, Ricardo, *A History of Argentina*. University of North Carolina Press, 1937.

Merriman, Roger Bigelow, *The Rise of the Spanish Empire in the Old World and the New*. Cooper Square Publishers, 4 vols., 1962.

Raine, Philip, *Paraguay*. Scarecrow Press, 1956.

Rojas, Ricardo, *San Martín*. Doubleday, Doran, 1945.

Ross, Gordon, *Argentina and Uruguay*. Macmillan, 1916.

Schurmann Pacheco, Mauricio, and Maria Luisa Coolighan Sanguinetti, *Historia del Uruguay*. A. Monteverde y Cía, Montevideo, 1960. *(Only in Spanish.)*

Street, John, *Artigas and the Emancipation of Uruguay*. Cambridge University Press, 1959.

Warren, Harris Gaylord, *Paraguay*. University of Oklahoma Press, 1949.

CHAPTER 5: MODERN PARAGUAY

Barrett, William E., *Woman on Horseback*. Frederick A. Stokes, 1938.

Durrell, Gerald, *The Drunken Forest*. The Viking Press, 1956.

Graham, R. B. Cunninghame, *Portrait of a Dictator: Francisco Solano López*. Heinemann, London, 1933. *A Vanished Arcadia*. Heinemann, London, 1901.

Pendle, George, *Paraguay*. Oxford University Press, 1956.

Raine, Philip, *Paraguay*. Scarecrow Press, 1956.

Service, Elman R. and Helen S., *Tobati, Paraguayan Town*. University of Chicago Press, 1954.

Social Progress Trust Fund—Third Annual Report, 1963. Inter-American Development Bank, 1963.

Warren, Harris Gaylord, *Paraguay*. University of Oklahoma Press, 1949.

Washburn, Charles A., *The History of Paraguay*. Lee and Shepard, 2 vols., 1871.

Zook, David H., Jr., *The Conduct of the Chaco War*. Bookman Associates, 1960.

CHAPTER 6: ARGENTINA AND PERÓN

Alexander, Robert J., *The Peron Era*. Columbia University Press, 1951.

Argentina 1930—1960. Sur, Buenos Aires, 1961.

Blanksten, George I., *Perón's Argentina*. University of Chicago Press, 1953.

Cowles, Fleur, *Bloody Precedent*. Random House, 1952.

Josephs, Ray, *Argentine Diary*. Random House, 1944.

Pendle, George, *Argentina*. Oxford University Press, 1963.

Romero, José Luis, *A History of Argentine Political Thought*. Stanford University Press, 1963.

Szulc, Tad, *Twilight of the Tyrants*. Henry Holt, 1959.

Whitaker, Arthur P., *Argentina*. Prentice-Hall, 1964. *Argentine Upheaval*. Frederick A. Praeger, 1956.

CHAPTER 7: URUGUAY'S DEMOCRACY

Alexander, Robert J., *Prophets of the Revolution*. Macmillan, 1962.

Fitzgibbon, Russell H., *Uruguay*. Rutgers University Press, 1954.

Hanson, Simon G., *Utopia in Uruguay*. Oxford University Press, 1938.

Hudson, W. H., *The Purple Land*. E. P. Dutton, 1927.

Northrop, F.S.C., *Philosophical Anthropology and Practical Politics*. Macmillan, 1960.

Pendle, George, *Uruguay*. Oxford University Press, 1963.

Taylor, Philip B., Jr., *Government and Politics of Uruguay*. Tulane University, 1960.

Vanger, Milton I., *José Batlle y Ordoñez of Uruguay*. Harvard University Press, 1963.

CHAPTER 8: THE POWER GROUPS

Fitzgibbon, Russell H., *Uruguay*. Rutgers University Press, 1954.

Haring, C. H., *The Spanish Empire in America*. Oxford University Press, 1947.

Johnson, John J., *The Military and Society in Latin America*. Stanford University Press, 1964.

Pendle, George, *Argentina*. Oxford University Press, 1963. *Uruguay*. Oxford University Press, 1963.

Raine, Philip, *Paraguay*. Scarecrow Press, 1956.

Scobie, James R., *Argentina; A City and a Nation*. Oxford University Press, 1964.

CHAPTER 9: THE ARTS

Anderson-Imbert, Enrique, *Spanish-American Literature*. Wayne State University Press, 1963.

Apel, Paul H., *Music of the Americas North and South*. Vantage Press, 1958.

Chase, Gilbert, *A Guide to the Music of Latin America*. The Pan American Union and The Library of Congress, 1962.

Crawford, William Rex, *A Century of Latin-American Thought*. Harvard University Press, 1961.

Fitts, Dudley, ed., *Anthology of Contemporary Latin-American Poetry*. New Directions, 1942.

Henríquez-Ureña, Pedro, *Literary Currents*

in Hispanic America. Harvard University Press, 1945.

Jones, Willis Knapp, *Spanish-American Literature in Translation.* Frederick Ungar, 1963.

Sanchez, Luis Alberto, *Nueva Historia de La Literatura Americana.* Editorial Americalee, Buenos Aires, 1943. *(Only in Spanish.)*

Slonimsky, Nicolas, *Music of Latin America.* Thomas Y. Crowell Company, 1945.

CHAPTER 10: WORLD WAR II AND AFTER

Bruce, James, *Those Perplexing Argentines.* Longmans, Green, 1953.

Clark, Gerald, *The Coming Explosion in Latin America.* David McKay Company, 1963.

Ferns, H. S., *Britain and Argentina in the Nineteenth Century.* Oxford University Press, 1960.

Fitzgibbon, Russell H., *Uruguay.* Rutgers University Press, 1954.

Houston, John A., *Latin America in the United Nations.* Carnegie Endowment for International Peace, 1956.

Kelly, Sir David, *The Ruling Few, or the Human Background to Diplomacy.* Hollis & Carter, London, 1953.

Peterson, Harold F., *Argentina and the United States—1810-1960.* State University of New York, 1964.

Rennie, Ysabel F., *The Argentine Republic.* Macmillan, 1945.

FAMOUS RIVER PLATE CULTURAL FIGURES AND THEIR PRINCIPAL WORKS

LITERATURE

Díaz de Guzmán, Ruy	c.1554-1629	Paraguayan. Early mestizo historian who wrote fancifully of the River Plate area
Echeverría, Esteban	1805-1851	Argentine. Exiled by dictator Rosas, he returned to Argentina to write the poem *"La cautiva"* (The Captive) and a prose sketch, *El matadero*
Sarmiento, Domingo Faustino	1811-1888	Argentine. Writer, educator and President of Argentina. *Facundo, Life in the Argentine Republic in the Days of the Tyrants*
Mármol, José	1817-1871	Argentine. A poet who also wrote dramas and novels. Novel: *Amalia*
Mitre, Bartolomé	1821-1906	Argentine. A President of Argentina, he wrote verse, essays, criticism and historical studies. *Historia de Belgrano*
Hernández, José	1834-1886	Argentine. Wrote the famous epic poem *The Gaucho Martín Fierro*
Zorrilla de San Martín, Juan	1855-1931	Uruguayan. Romantic and patriotic poetry. *La leyenda patria, Tabaré*
Alonso y Trelles, José	1857-1924	Uruguayan. Born in Spain, he wrote of Gauchos in verse under the pen name of *"El Viejo Pancho"*
Viana, Javier de	1868-1926	Uruguayan. Prolific and forceful prose writer. Novel: *Gaucha*
Rodó, José Enrique	1871-1917	Uruguayan. Writer of philosophical essays, notably *Ariel*
Vaz Ferreira, Carlos	1873-1958	Uruguayan. Original thinker, humanist and educator. *Fermentario*
Larreta, Enrique	1873-1961	Argentine. Historical novel: *La gloria de don Ramiro*
Lugones, Leopoldo	1874-1938	Argentine. Modernist poet and prose writer. Poems: *Montañas del oro.* Criticism: *Historia de Sarmiento.* Fantastic tales: *Las fuerzas extrañas*
Herrera y Reissig, Julio	1875-1910	Uruguayan. Outstanding symbolist poet. *Pascuas del tiempo, "Los carros"*
Sánchez, Florencio	1875-1910	Uruguayan. Prolific playwright. Realistic rural drama: *La Gringa*
Quiroga, Horacio	1878-1937	Uruguayan. Short stories of life on the upper Paraná River: *Cuentos de la selva, "El hijo"*
Lynch, Benito	1880-1951	Argentine. Popular novelist who wrote evocative descriptions of rural Argentine society: *El inglés de los güesos*
Rojas, Ricardo	1882-1957	Argentine. Poet, short-story writer, essayist and historian. Biographies of San Martín and Sarmiento. *La restauración nacionalista, La argentinidad*
Gálvez, Manuel	1882-1962	Argentine. Realistic novels including *El mal metafísico, Tránsito Guzmán*
Agustini, Delmira	1886-1914	Uruguayan. Sensual lyric poet. *El libro blanco, Los astros del abismo*
Güiraldes, Ricardo	1886-1927	Argentine. Intellectual poet and author of the Gaucho novel *Don Segundo Sombra*
Sabat Ercasty, Carlos	1887-	Uruguayan. Poet who has written on the unity of God and creation. *Pantheos*
Zum Felde, Alberto	1888-	Uruguayan. Social historian and literary critic. *Proceso intelectual del Uruguay*
Romero, Francisco	1891-1962	Argentine. Philosopher and elegant stylist. *Teoría del hombre*
Storni, Alfonsina	1892-1938	Argentine. Swiss-born poet whose works are concerned with nature, death and the transmigration of the soul. *El dulce daño, El mundo de siete pozos*
Ocampo, Victoria	1893-	Argentine. Editor, publisher and writer. Autobiography: *Testimonios.* An interpretation of T. E. Lawrence: *338171 T. E.*
Eichelbaum, Samuel	1894-	Argentine. Somber analytical dramas: *Pájaro de barro, Dos brasas*
Ibarbourou, Juana	1895-	Uruguayan. Poems dealing with both pagan sensuality and the pleasures of family life: *Las lenguas de diamente, La rosa de los vientos*
Martínez Estrada, Ezequiel	1895-	Argentine. Poet and prose writer. *Ora y piedra, Humoresca, Radiografía de la Pampa*
González, Natalicio	1897-	Paraguayan. Poet, historian, politician and educator. Poems: *Baladas guaraníes*
Molinari, Ricardo E.	1898-	Argentine. Poet whose odes reveal his Spanish classicist education. *Unida noche*
Borges, Jorge Luis	1899-	Argentine. Outstanding literary figure. Poetry, stories, novels and essays. Poems: *Fervor de Buenos Aires.* Stories and essays: *Labyrinths, Ficciones, Dreamtigers*
Arlt, Roberto	1900-1942	Argentine. Dostoevskian novelist of the frustrated hopes of the middle class. *El juguete rabioso, Los siete locos*
Mallea, Eduardo	1903-	Argentine. Prose writer who examines the moral condition of his country. *Historia de una Pasión Argentina, Nocturno europeo.* Short stories and sketches
Casaccia, Gabriel	1907-	Paraguayan. Powerful novel of Paraguayan village life: *La babosa*
Campos Cervera, Herib	1908-1953	Paraguayan. Poems on war, politics, labor and nostalgia. *Ceniza redimida*

Pla, Josefina	1909-	Paraguayan. Poet, playwright and critic born in the Canary Islands. *El precio de los sueños, La raíz y la aurora*
Sábato, Ernesto	1911-	Argentine. Highly regarded essayist and novelist. *The Tunnel, Sobre héroes y tumbas*
Bioy Casares, Adolfo	1914-	Argentine. Novelist who describes fabulous worlds. *El sueño de los héroes, The Invention of Morel and Other Stories*
Wéyland, W.G. (Silverio Boj)	c.1914-	Argentine. Fiction writer. *Belgrano "R," Aspero intermedio*
Cortázar, Julio	1916-	Argentine. Novels examining sham in life and literature: *The Winner, Rayuela*
Roa Bastos, Augusto	1918-	Paraguayan. Representative poet and novelist whose prose is mixture of Spanish and Guarani. Novels: *Hijo de hombre, El trueno entre las hojas*
Denevi, Marco	1922-	Argentine. Compelling psychological novel of murder: *Rosa at Ten O'Clock*
Murena, Héctor A.	1923-	Argentine. Writes poetry, essays and novels. One of the definers of his generation. Trilogy: *Historia de un día*

MUSIC

Williams, Alberto	1862-1952	Argentine. The patriarch of Argentine music. Symphonies, choral works, sonatas and chamber music
Buchardo, Carlos López	1881-	Argentine. Has composed orchestral and vocal music inspired by native themes. *Escenas argentinas*. Opera: *El sueño de Alma*
Fabini, Eduardo	1883-1951	Uruguayan. Orchestral music of native inspiration: *Isla de los ciebos*. Ballet: *Mburucuyá*
Gilardi, Gilardo	1889-1963	Argentine. Vocal and theater music: *Ilse, La leyenda de Urutaú*
Palma, Athos	1891-1951	Argentine. Symphonic poems: *Los hijos del sol, Jardines*
Castro, José María	1892-1964	Argentine. Neoromantic orchestral and vocal music. *Sonata de primavera*
Castro, Juan José	1895-	Argentine. Symphonic music written in a neoclassic style. *Sinfonía argentina*
Gianneo, Luis	1897-	Argentine. Folkloric pieces in modern idiom. *Concierto Aymará*. Symphonic poem: *Turay-Turay*
Flores, José Asunción	1904-	Paraguayan. Created a new musical form, the *Guaranía*, raising native rhythms to new artistic levels
Estrada, Carlos	1909-1964	Uruguayan. Composer of lyrical songs. *Caminos tristes*
Morillo, García Roberto	1911-	Argentine. Composer influenced by Russian music. Piano suite: *Conjuros*. Ballet: *Harrild*
Moreno, Juan Carlos	1912-	Paraguayan. First composer to use native Paraguayan themes in established musical forms
Ginastera, Alberto	1916-	Argentine. Latin America's outstanding composer. His works include symphonies, concertos, chamber music and scores composed for both films and the stage. *Panambí, Concierto argentino, Sinfonía de "Don Rodrigo," Bomarzo*
Tozar, Héctor	1923-	Uruguayan. Neoclassic composer who uses native themes. *Toccata, Danza criolla*

PAINTING AND SCULPTURE

Morel, Carlos	1813-1894	Argentine. The first Argentine-born painter of note. Portraits and battle scenes: *Cavalry Action in Rosas' Time*
Pueyrredón, Prilidiano	1823-1870	Argentine. An early painter of portraits and landscapes. *The Meeting of the Gauchos, A Stop on the Way*
Sívori, Eduardo	1847-1918	Argentine. One of the first Argentine painters trained in Europe. *The Pampa in Olavarría, Le Lever de la Bonne, Portrait*
Mendilharzu, Graciano	1857-1894	Argentine. Painter who studied under Bonnat in Paris. *Coming Home, Portrait of Don Carlos Vega Belgrano, The Prostitute's Dinner*
Figari, Pedro	1861-1938	Uruguayan. Painter, philosopher, lawyer and diplomat. Monumental text on esthetics: *El Arte, la estética y el ideal*
Torres García, Joaquín	1874-1949	Uruguayan. Painter with a highly personal style. *Monumento cósmico, Composition, Pintura constructiva*
Daneri, Eugenio	1881-	Argentine. Painter of landscapes and still lifes. *Old Houses in La Boca, The Loss of the Son, Figure*
Fader, Fernando	1882-1935	Argentine. Used Expressionist techniques in such paintings as *Nude before the Stove, Oxen Plowing, The Manila Shawls*
Belloni, José	1882-	Uruguayan. Unofficial sculptor-laureate of Uruguay. *La carreta, La diligencia*
Pettoruti, Emilio	1892-	Argentine. Painter whose works blend Futurist and Cubist styles. *Autumn Sun, The Verdigris Goblet, The Bouquet*
Butler, Horacio	1897-	Argentine. Painter, stage designer, illustrator. *Afternoon in El Tigre, El camelote: Tigre, Passage*
Forner, Raquel	1902-	Argentine. Paintings which are often allegorical, sometimes tending toward Surrealism. *Desolation, The Bull in Red, Apocalypsis*
Fernández-Muro, Juan Antonio	1920-	Argentine. Outstanding present-day painter in Argentina. *Composition, Red over Grey, Scarlet Medal, Reflecting the Surface, Silvered Circle*
Grilo, Sarah	1920-	Argentine. Nonobjective painter who lives and works in New York. *Red and Blue, Three Circles, January 1963, Charge*
Páez Vilaró, Carlos	1923-	Uruguayan. Self-taught painter of murals. His works include the world's longest mural, *Roots of Peace*, in the Pan American Union Building, Washington, D.C.
Kazuya, Sakai	1927-	Argentine. Painter of Japanese extraction. *Jyoshu's "Mu," Little Theatre*
Bonevardi, Marcelo	1929-	Argentine. Painter whose *Astrologer's Table* suggests sculptured construction in wood
Macció, Rómulo	1931-	Argentine. Self-taught painter. *To Live: Without a Guarantee, To Live: By Leaps and Bounds*

Credits

The sources for the illustrations in this book appear below. Credits for pictures from left to right are separated by commas, from top to bottom by dashes.

Cover—Leonard McCombe

8, 9—Leonard McCombe

10—Map by Rafael Palacios

13—Map by Rafael Palacios

16 through 24—Leonard McCombe

32 through 45—Leonard McCombe

53 through 59—Leonard McCombe

60, 61—Culver Pictures

62—left, Radio Times Hulton Picture Library

63—Culver Pictures

69—Leonard McCombe

70—Leonard McCombe—Frank Scherschel

71 through 77—Leonard McCombe

81 through 87—Leonard McCombe

88, 89—*Paris-Match*

98, 99—Thomas D. McAvoy, Gisele Freund from Magnum

100, 101—center and right, Cornell Capa from Magnum; bottom left, Hank Walker

102—top, Service Grafico Schneider-De Linden

103—Cornell Capa from Magnum

104—Leonard McCombe

107—Drawing adapted by Mark Binn courtesy Culver Pictures

110 through 119—Leonard McCombe

125—Francisco Vera

126, 127—Francisco Vera except top center Paulo Muniz and right Leonard McCombe

128 through 132—Leonard McCombe

139—Leonard McCombe except bottom Francisco Vera

140, 141—Leonard McCombe

142—Charles Uht Private Collection, New York—Charles Uht

143, 144—Leonard McCombe

149, 150, 151—Leonard McCombe

ACKNOWLEDGMENTS

The editors wish to express their appreciation to Lewis Hanke, Professor of Latin American History, Columbia University, who read and commented on the entire text; and to Gregory Rabassa, Associate Professor of Spanish and Portuguese, Columbia University, who gave special assistance with portions of the text.

Index

This symbol in front of a page number indicates a photograph or painting of the subject mentioned.

Production staff for Time Incorporated

Arthur R. Murphy Jr. (Vice President and Director of Production)

Robert E. Foy, James P. Menton, Caroline Ferri and Robert E. Fraser

Text photocomposed under the direction of

Albert J. Dunn and Arthur J. Dunn

x

Printed by R. R. Donnelley & Sons Company, Crawfordsville, Indiana

and The Safran Printing Company, Detroit, Michigan

Bound by R. R. Donnelley & Sons Company, Crawfordsville, Indiana

Paper by The Mead Corporation, Dayton, Ohio

Cover stock by The Plastic Coating Corporation, Holyoke, Massachusetts

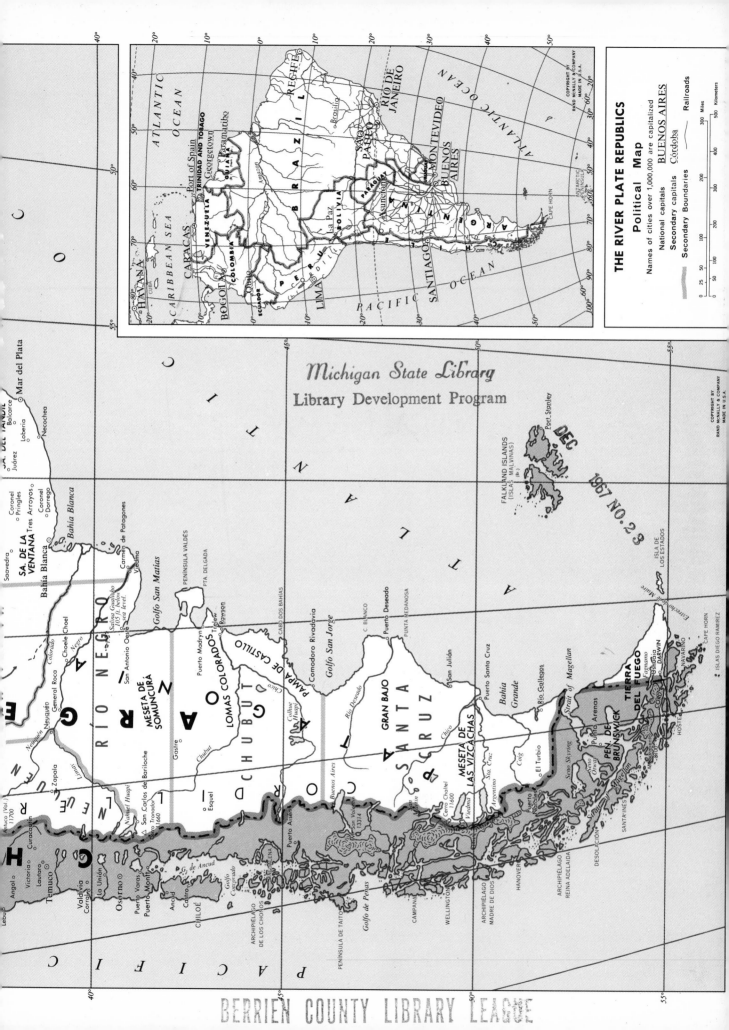